HOW TO WIN OVER

Loneliness

JOHN HAGGAI

HARVEST HOUSE PUBLISHERS
Eugene, Oregon 97402

Except where otherwise indicated all Scripture quotations in this book are taken from the King James Version of the Bible.

HOW TO WIN OVER LONELINESS

Copyright © 1988 by John E. Haggai
Published by Harvest House Publishers
Eugene, Oregon 97402

Library of Congress Cataloging-in-Publication Data

Haggai, John Edmund.
  How to win over loneliness.

     1. Loneliness—Religious aspects—Christianity.
I. Title.
BV4911.H33   1988   248.8'6   88-80061
ISBN 0-89081-689-1 (pbk.)

HOW TO
WIN
OVER

Loneliness

Contents

Part 1

GET READY, GET RIGHT

1

Alone Together

It may surprise you to read that I've known a lot of loneliness in my life.

In my youth loneliness sprang from being weak and timid. I didn't walk until I was over two, and didn't talk until nearly three. When I did talk I was so shy that I remember my father threatening to punish me if I didn't come out and speak to guests in our home. Some of that shyness has hung on. Even now, if I see a group of friends standing in a hotel lobby—friends I love and respect—I find it easier to slip by unnoticed than go and talk to them.

As a child, timidity cut me off from other people. I was embarrassed by displays of emotion. When I walked into the living room as a six-year-old to find my parents hugging each other I mumbled, "Oh, excuse me!" and retired in a hurry! If I was the one being hugged my discomfort was worse still—in fact my parents became so conscious of this that when it came to physical expressions of love like kissing and embracing they treated me with greater caution than they did my brothers Ted and Tom.

Unaware that I was the cause of the problem, I concluded that since I received the fewest hugs I was the least loved member of the family and must therefore have been adopted. At eight, I recall, I was spending long, lonely hours comforting myself with the thought that, if I wasn't loved, I sure was lucky to have such a good home. Adopted I might be, but at least I wasn't out on the street.

And then in 1932 I got some good news. My teacher in the third grade explained to us that when we were born a birth certificate was made out, giving all the relevant details about parents, age, sex, weight, and the time and place of birth. I was overjoyed, and rushed home to confront my mother.

But my mother seemed strangely evasive.

"John Edmund," she said, "it's interesting you should ask about that because I have been trying to get your birth certificate. You see, the doctor who delivered you has died, and there were some irregularities in the record-keeping. But I have been working for some time on getting the certificate."

Hope crumbled. "She's hiding something from me," I thought. "Now I know I'm adopted."

I hardly listened to her as she described to me the circumstances of my birth, in the Susan Speed Hospital in Louisville, Kentucky, on February 27, 1924. I wasn't impressed that she knew the doctor's name. I felt utterly crushed, and I went on feeling that way until, several weeks later and out of the blue, my mother remarked, "Oh, John Edmund, your birth certificate came in the mail today." I grasped that piece of paper as though it were a stay of execution. And the next time I looked in the mirror I noticed for the first time the similarities between myself and my parents.

The Lonely Schoolboy

But that didn't solve the loneliness problem. At the age of 13 I was sent on a generous scholarship to Stony Brook School for Boys. Only pride prevented me from letting on how frightened I was. Many of the students came from far richer homes than mine (the Susan Speed Hospital where I had been born was run by the Salvation Army for the benefit of the poor). They had fine clothes. Some even drove automobiles. I hoped my parents were going to stay through the first lunch hour, but while sitting in the introductory Latin class I heard the old 1930 Chevrolet grinding away down the drive in second gear.

I don't think I'd ever been lonelier. My total cash flow was four dollars, and it had to last until Christmas. There was no possibility of buying sports gear, taking bus trips into neighboring towns, or getting tickets for athletic events. When Thanksgiving came around I was one of the handful of students anchored at school because there was no money for the trip home.

The fact that my roommate was the son of a missionary gave me no consolation. He was five-feet-six and I was four-feet-eleven. I realize now that he was a good boy with high ideals and deep convictions, but at the time his nagging got on my nerves, and during one study time when he got on to me about something, I ended up landing an uppercut on his jaw. That was the only way I could reach him!

I immediately felt ashamed and humiliated—most of all because I had knocked the gold cap off one of his front teeth. Of course I offered to pay for the repair. As the son of a minister who worked sometimes at starvation wages, I was sensitive to the economic limitations of missionaries. The boy's parents graciously agreed to my offer, and I set to work to raise the money. Fortunately I had just begun a little sideline selling neckties. I still remember the slogan:

BE WISE
ECONOMIZE
BUY A TIE
FROM HAGGAI!

Those early years at the school were trying in many ways. I was physically weak. I had a high, grating voice. I was hopelessly shy. I bore the unmistakable imprint of my father's Syrian extraction. And on top of everything else I was known as a preacher's kid. To a boy my age that spelled one word—loneliness.

One day the school got a visit from a famous world missionary statesman, Dr. John R. Mott. The address which this 70-year-old man delivered in the chapel, on "The Temptations of Youth," was utterly humorless. But it held every student on the edge of his seat. The whole school was spellbound. When the dean announced afterward that Dr. Mott had agreed to give counseling in 15-minute slots to as many boys as his schedule permitted him to see, there was a rush to get into the line. I would have given a lot for 15 minutes with Dr. Mott, but being small and slow I came up at the end of the line and never got to see him.

My loneliness deepened.

At last I decided that the only way to make myself more acceptable to my peers was to get in shape physically. I took up wrestling. It didn't go well at first. I was light, and an AAU champion in the 145-pound division managed to break my collarbone while teaching me a new hold. That put me out of commission for several weeks. But I persevered, and by the age of 15 I was doing body-building, weight-lifting, and acrobatic gymnastics.

These helped me a lot. The turning point, though, came in my senior year, when I got laid up in bed for several weeks following an automobile accident. My mother gave me a book that changed the course of my life. The writer urged his readers to seek out people of outstanding achievement, to make friends with them, to learn from them and be inspired by them. The thought came to me that I had been trying to develop in a vacuum. So wrapped up had I become in my own sense of inferiority that I had neglected to take the initiative in making friends. I determined to take the writer's advice to heart, and since that time I have always made it a habit to aggressively develop friendships.

My Deepest Loneliness

Did that put an end to loneliness? Well, not really. One of my young colleagues—in his thirties and the father of three precious children—said to me recently, "John, don't you get terribly lonesome on your travels? When I'm away from my family for two hours, I get so lonely I can hardly stand it."

My first response was, "Michael, the Lord has blessed me with so much hay on my fork, so much work to get done, so many deadlines to meet, that I don't have time to think about it."

But later, as I pondered his question, I had to confess that there have been times when I felt terribly lonely. My salvation lies in the fact that (as I said to Michael) I am usually immersed in work and service. Nonetheless, if I am honest I cannot deny that even as a Christian, and even after adopting various stratagems against it (such as making friends), I have still been afflicted with the experience of loneliness. It has been there in my constant traveling and my separation from the ones I love. Most of all it has hit me in the death of my son, Johnny, an invalid for 24 years, whose story I have already told in another book.

Many times when I was traveling on the other side of the world I would think about those awful seizures he had. I don't know how often we had to grab him up, bundle him into a car, and race him to the hospital to get emergency medication. The horror of that experience used to play like a movie on the screen of my mind. Every time it happened a quiet terror plagued me: "What will Chris do if this happens while I'm gone?"

In fact Chris, my wife, always coped admirably. But somehow that never relieved my own sense of pressure and loneliness. Only God knows the sickness I felt in the pit of my stomach when I had to leave the house on yet another trip. If I were prone to ulcers, my stomach would be full of them by now.

For 24 years we lived like that. I hated to be away from home. I even felt guilty that I wasn't doing for Johnny what I felt needed to be done. But I knew it would neither glorify God nor help Johnny and Chris if I abandoned my spiritual responsibilities. They freed me up to serve God, and I believe that God ministered to them in ways they may not even have realized.

My loneliness with Johnny entered a whole new phase when the Lord took him home, in 1975. Sooner or later everyone has to deal with the loneliness of bereavement. Many would say that it is the deepest kind of loneliness. I must admit I miss Johnny intensely. He was our only child, and although he needed constant attention and never managed to speak more than two intelligible words, I could not have asked for a more loving or supportive son. I found such great release in sharing with him the joys and difficulties of my ministry. I knew I could rely on him to pray for me. Not a day passes now when I do not think of him, or wish I could still share my dreams and watch his eyes light up in response to a new idea.

But I can't. He's gone. And much of what I have learned about winning over loneliness I have learned by facing this, my own deepest loneliness.

Loneliness and You

So I've been lonely. And you've been lonely, too. Probably that's why you're reading this book now. It's nothing to be ashamed of. Every human being has experienced loneliness at some time. And just as we all lead different lives, so our encounters with loneliness vary. It arises through crises as well as through the ordinary course of daily life. No two people are lonely in quite the same way or for quite the same reason, though there are common themes in loneliness that we will be looking at in the next chapter.

The point I want to make here is that loneliness simply as an experience—an unpleasant feeling we don't like—should be classified as a *pain*. Like every other pain, it came into the world through the fall of man. Like every other pain, it hurts us. We are not necessarily sinning against God or letting Him down if we seek relief in tears; if my background had permitted me to cry, I know that crying would sometimes have brought comfort in loneliness. Loneliness is a pain that we should not have to endure in a perfect world, and in fact we shall not endure it in the world to come.* Most important of all, it is a pain we can conquer by using the methods which God directed me to employ in confronting loneliness, and which I am going to pass on to you.

But there is something else about loneliness that you need to know right at the start of this book. Loneliness per se is not a sin. But it is a complex phenomenon, often embracing

---

* For further help on pain in general, see the companion volume to this, entitled *How to Win Over Pain*.

a wide range of other experiences, such as boredom, isolation, frustration, emptiness, and low self-image. And it is dangerous—a destructive force that can easily bind the sufferer into a state of sin before he or she actually realizes it. When this happens, and loneliness is permitted to persist, to run wild and unchecked, it will destroy the lonely person and greatly harm those who are close by. For that reason it is vital to confront loneliness; it is a progressive condition that can distort and undermine our personality, and it must be tackled promptly.

2

Five Ways to Be Lonely

Western society has many misconceptions about loneliness. The most common one is that loneliness is the same as solitude.

It's not.

Solitude is defined in Webster's dictionary as "the quality or state of being alone." No one will deny that seclusion can be an *ingredient* of loneliness, but it isn't always so, and in fact the two concepts are quite different. This can be proven from experience. Many of the world's happiest and most fulfilled people have enjoyed solitude. Daniel Boone, the American frontiersman, loved to be alone. So did Madame Curie and Henry Ford. Conversely, President Warren G. Harding, who was surrounded by people 24 hours a day, said he felt imprisoned in the White House and terrifyingly lonely.

In other words, you can be alone without being lonely and lonely without being alone.

This is true even in the case of enforced solitude, or solitary confinement. In an interview in 1978, the late President Anwar Sadat of Egypt said that his six months in solitary confinement constituted the greatest period of his life. In such a situation, he said, you really get to know who you are. Much the same point was made by Admiral James Bond Stockdale, President of the Naval War College in Annapolis, who was a prisoner of war for 7½ years in Vietnam, four of them in solitary confinement. He admitted it was tough to start with:

> After the first week or two you do think you are going to go crazy; but after a year or two, with all of the mental gymnastics, plans, prayers, you hardly have enough time. You go to bed disappointed that you didn't have more time. Solitude is a good way to live after you get used to it.

17

He claims that the common fear of going crazy from being alone arises from "the modern proliferation of entertainment." Against this, his POW experience gave him a "sense of proportion" and even contained "some of the happiest days of my life."

Similarly, loneliness is not the same as a solitary lifestyle. Newscaster Paul Harvey forgoes most normal socializing. He has to go to bed at eight so he can be in his office in Chicago's Loop before five in the morning. But that doesn't make him feel lonely. On the contrary, when he gets home he often spends his afternoons on his own in his workshop, building model airplanes.

So whatever circumstance it is that separates a person from his or her normal social circle, the resulting experience of solitude is not to be identified with loneliness. The two are completely different, even when they occur together. In the same way it is wrong to call depression or inadequacy "loneliness." Depression can be the cause of loneliness or the result of it, but it is not the *same* as loneliness. As for feelings of inadequacy, can you imagine someone more inadequate for social life than Helen Keller? Yet the biography of this woman, who remained until her dying day a blind deaf-mute, gives not the remotest hint that she was lonely.

The reason why loneliness and solitude are different is actually quite simple.

Solitude has to do with physical location. You are alone because your situation or your schedule is such that interaction with other people is restricted. Say you're a housewife whose family has flown the nest, or you've had an accident and you're lying in the hospital. In either case you will spend much of your time in solitude. But you will not feel lonely as long as that solitude *leaves your most important relationships intact*. Loneliness, you see, is not a lack of *interaction* but a lack of *relationship*. That is why a noted psychologist has said that loneliness "does not come from having no people about one, but from holding certain views that others find inadmissible." Of course having unpopular opinions isn't the only thing that will destroy your relationships. Still, his point is sound: Loneliness isn't simply solitude—it's *unwanted* solitude, solitude arising out of broken relationships, a solitude that we might term "emotional isolation."

Right relationships are the one solid foundation of human happiness and fulfillment (I will explore this idea a little later). *Which* missing relationships will result in your feeling lonely depends on which relationships are most important to you. None of us will feel lonely for a person we've only met once, because such a casual encounter will hardly ever sustain an important relationship. On the other hand, loss of contact with close friends, and more especially with family, has a strong potential for causing emotional isolation.

You may have only one or two important relationships in your life, or you may have several. It depends on what kind of person you are. But I emphasize that when I talk about relationships I don't only mean relationships with other people. The most important relationship of all is the one you have with God. John the Baptist is an example of a man who had almost no other important relationships in his life besides his relationship with God. But he didn't experience loneliness. Nor did Jesus—except perhaps for one momentous instant on the cross when, bearing the weight of human sin, it felt to Him as though the Father Himself had turned away from Him:

> About the ninth hour Jesus cried with a loud voice, saying, "Eli, Eli, lama sabachthani?" that is to say, "My God, my God, why hast thou forsaken me?" (Matthew 27:46).

But more about that later. For now I want to concentrate on the way in which deficient or missing relationships produce different types of loneliness.

The Loneliness Syndrome

Loneliness is a universal experience. Everyone from the Hollywood film star to the unsophisticated tribesman in central Borneo knows what it's like to feel emotionally isolated.

But this is not to say that the experience never varies. It occurs in different forms and for different reasons. Compare the loneliness of the refugee fleeing from drought in East Africa to that of the elderly pensioner in Great Britain, the loneliness of the middle-aged housewife to that of the executive who travels from hotel to hotel. It's like the same play staged in different theaters, with different scenery and different actors.

What is true of location in space is also true of location in time. People described in the Bible, in the Greek and Roman classics, and in ancient Eastern literature clearly had encounters with loneliness quite similar to ours today. The Oxford English Dictionary dates the use of the English word "lonely," in the sense of "sad at being alone," from a line written by Byron in 1811. But it is significant of a change in the consciousness of the Western world that the noun "loneliness" did not acquire its present meaning until this century, and did not appear in any major dictionary until after the Second World War. In other words, loneliness has only recently been thought of as a mental condition or "syndrome."

The social trends underlying this change can be seen clearly in the United States. Just look at the classified pages in your newspaper. You'll find advertisements for sensitivity groups, singles apartments, and multimillion-dollar dating services. In fact the evidence is staring at you in every part of the media. Loneliness is now a major theme in the songs Americans sing and in the poems and books they write. It pushes housewives out in droves to find employment, and husbands into an unbalanced obsession with work. It is written large in the steady rise in rates of divorce, of child defection, and of suicide.

As a leader of the developed world, America typifies a change that is happening, to a greater or lesser extent, in all countries affected by Western outlooks and lifestyles. But why is it happening? And why do we find loneliness such a problem?

In an article in *Family Circle* in 1978, Suzanne Gordon, author of the book *Lonely in America*, blamed loneliness on the new ethic of individual fulfillment. Doing "my thing," she argued, has become such an obsession that doing "our thing" is virtually impossible.

Look at the American of the early nineteenth century and you'll see a person entirely inner-directed. He had a system of values that would not bend to the whims of his environment or be affected by the attitude of his peer group. Indeed, this peer group often reinforced his values. He was accustomed to solitude as well. As one of America's top sociologists, Pitirim Sorokin, has said: "Facing loneliness was once a mark of manhood in American civilization. In an earlier era, Americans were reared to face life on their own in the struggle to achieve success through work." In fact being alone, he goes on to suggest, was part of the definition of successful living.

By the middle of the century, however, these absolute values were being undermined by rapid and violent social change. Convictions didn't "pay" in the way they once had. Industrialization and urbanization redefined the citizen's economic role. He was no longer engaged in the task of mastering the physical environment—or at least only in his backyard. Instead, he set about "earning a living." Success in this new situation depended less on strength and resourcefulness than on a talent for currying favor. The new American man learned how to win friends and influence people.

In these circumstances, inflexible principles and contempt for public opinion were a liability, not an asset. The damaging adjustment began. Conscience ceased to be the governing factor in a person's action or opinion. Its place was taken by the urge to conform to current trends, to ensure at all costs that behavior, outlook, and lifestyle were acceptable to the peer group. As one commentator has put it, to find out what a modern American thinks you need only know the last book he read or the last TV program he viewed.

By this analysis it is hardly surprising that loneliness has become a particular problem in American society. The individual feels that he is in constant danger of losing his place in the estimation of his peers. He feels lonely in the crowd because he can never be sure that his ideas, values, and opinions are the ones that happen to be in vogue. Each morning he is threatened with the fate of becoming yesterday's man. He suffers loneliness in anticipation of being rejected by those on whom he depends for his livelihood and his emotional support, even when they have not rejected him. Worse still, it is a loneliness with a double edge, because now that he has no value system of his own, his acceptance by others is his only measure of personal success. So if he is indeed rejected as he fears, he is not only made lonely but is proven to be a failure.

The theory is borne out by the facts. Psychiatrists do not only philosophize on the causes of the modern neurosis; they provide any number of concepts, formulas, and clinics through which the sufferer—if he has the money—can seek a cure. Marin County in California, surely one of the world's wealthier neighborhoods, is reported to have a psychiatrist for every 200 citizens! I believe that this plethora of counselors and therapists has actually made the situation worse. Their credentialed leaders are right to censure the dominant pop psychology, but too often the only replacement they can offer is some fad of their own.

My brother Tom is now on 400 radio stations daily across America. His sole purpose is to give people a lift in his daily five-minute broadcast which he calls "Values for Better Living." He does not solicit mail. He never offers a premium, never asks for funds. Yet he receives a constant stream of letters in which loneliness figures more highly than any other single topic. Apparently it causes as much concern to students at Ohio State University as it does to retired people on the west coast of Florida. He said to me recently:

> I think it is the biggest problem facing our nation.
> I don't know any problem that equals it. The fact
> that the people who write us have to go to a certain
> amount of trouble to find out where to address us
> and how to get in touch with us indicates that they

feel deeply about this problem. I think it is the most deadly problem we have . . . far more deadly than inflation. People can somehow cope with inflation, no matter how painfully. True, it can destroy an economy. Yet the economy can be built back. You can't do a thing if there is not a feeling of purpose in life. The lonely feeling, the feeling of being neglected which is so prevalent in the lives of Americans, is a devastating and destructive force. . . .

Five Lonely People

Loneliness is a symptom of wrong relationships. But relationships can be broken in all sorts of ways, and so all sorts of loneliness can result. Does this mean that it is impossible to classify varieties of loneliness? I believe the answer is no. If you look at any society you will generally find five kinds of lonely people. Not everyone in a given group will be the same or find himself (or herself) in exactly the same situation—far from it. But members of one group will certainly have one characteristic in common—a characteristic connecting their relationships to their loneliness. I have given each group a name to indicate that connection and have supplied examples to show what kind of person might be found in that group. For convenience I have used the universal pronoun "he" to refer to both men and women.

Read the rest of this chapter carefully. One of these five lonely people is you.

1. *The Sandgrain*. This is the person whose loneliness results directly from solitude—physical or emotional, real or imagined. In many instances he is literally on his own. He may be confined to his house through illness or engaged in some long-term research project that takes him to lonely places. He may simply have a job with unsocial hours—perhaps as a night watchman at a warehouse. Any long-term situation of this kind can exert a pressure to feel lonely if the person concerned is not accustomed to solitude. The pressure

is even stronger if it stems from a sudden change in circumstances—for example, the death of a wife or husband or of anyone else who up till this time has played a major part in the person's social life.

Because loneliness is a matter of emotional and not just physical isolation, the Sandgrain is liable to feel lonely even when surrounded by other people. He is not actually suffering rejection by others, but something in his own circumstances or personality deprives him of the power to form relationships properly. This was my dilemma as a child. I had two parents and two brothers, all of whom loved me. But somehow I wasn't able to make those relationships count. I always imagined that, although I was treated with great generosity and respect, I wasn't actually loved. That was enough to make me lonely.

Others who feel that way really *aren't* loved. The traveling executive may not have time to establish deep and rewarding relationships. The exile, the new immigrant, the newly-moved-in, the missionary, the child beginning life at a different school—all of these may experience loneliness simply because they do not have the opportunity or the means to make proper social contacts. It isn't rejection on the part of others that makes them experience emotional isolation; they are not loved because they are not noticed.

If the Sandgrain is elderly, loneliness may hit him in a special way—through nostalgia. The person who retires to Florida may feel lonely at Christmastime for the snow and the sleigh and the caroling in the old hometown up north. The sights and sounds and values of yesteryear seem to have been cruelly swept aside by progress. The milk is no longer delivered by horse and wagon in the early hours; his principles and patriotism seem out of date, and are sometimes even derided on television shows. He wishes things could have stayed the way they were.

Of course nostalgia doesn't only affect those who are getting on in years. Some would deny that it is really a form of loneliness. But the fact is that we have relationships with places and periods as well as with people, and when these slip into our past we miss them just as we miss old friends. It even happens in churches to the older members who can remember the good old days before the pastor brought another 2000 people into the congregation! The isolation is from times and places, but it is isolation nonetheless.

2. *The Outsider.* This is the person whose loneliness results from actual rejection by other people.

There are a thousand and one ways of suffering rejection. In some instances we can take it. Most of us can put up with being disliked by one set of people if we know we are loved by another set. It comes back once again to which relationships are the most important to us. Only when those key relationships fail do we start to feel the pinch: the schoolgirl who is given the cold shoulder by her former friends; the wife abandoned by the man who a few short years before had vowed to love and cherish her; the child whose divorced parent has married again and who now feels like an intruder in the new home.

The child Outsider, rejected or ignored by his parents, can feel an almost-intolerable loneliness. A boy may work diligently to get good grades or succeed at Little League baseball or scouting. But if the father does not show appreciation the boy's spirit can be crushed. Too often a father gives his son the impression that success is only what is expected. Consequently no encouragement is given—only chastisement when the child fails to perform. At this point unfavorable comparison may be made with the boy's friends, or with an elder brother or sister who has blazed a trail of academic glory which the child is unable to follow. The effect is destructive. The child begins to feel isolated, and psychological mines are laid that in the best cases damage the child's self-image and in the worst cases completely explode the relationship.

Given our dislike of rejection, you might think that nobody in his right mind would voluntarily take on any kind of social handicap. But in fact the Outsider frequently does so, not out of perversity but by the dictate of conscience.

The Christian young lady who stands solidly on her biblical convictions often stands alone. She won't sleep around, she won't experiment with drugs, she won't drink or gamble or wear immodest clothing. By the standards prevailing among the young in today's America she will appear prudish, a killjoy. She may be ostracized and feel that she is unattractive to the opposite sex. If so, the temptation to compromise her convictions in order to get the attention of some eligible young man can nearly devastate her.

This experience of rejection for the sake of conscience is something that Jesus Himself endured. And He was completely candid about the prospects in store for His disciples:

> If ye were of the world, the world would love his own; but because ye are not of the world, but I have chosen you out of the world, therefore the world hateth you. Remember the word that I said unto you, "The servant is not greater than his lord." If they have persecuted me, they will also persecute you (John 15:19,20).

Such loneliness is part of the cost that many people count when they stand on the brink of the kingdom.

A few years ago an American celebrity came to share his tale of woe with a dear friend of mine, a prominent Manhattan pastor. When the pastor advised him to make a clean break and commit his life to Christ, he wept. He said, "To get to my present position I made certain commitments to people who propelled me to the top—commitments that are unbreakable. My life wouldn't be worth a thread over a flame if I were to make a commitment to Jesus Christ and follow through with a lifestyle that honors Him. They would kill me."

It isn't always high personal standards that make the Outsider unpopular. Depending on the time and place, it might be his political views, his socioeconomic class, or the color of his skin. Any of these can make him an outcast—and that means loneliness.

3. *The Lonely-in-Love*. Loneliness can exist not just in the presence of other people but also in the context of an established relationship. Marriage is the clearest example. Imagine a person who has been married several years, has had children, and shares a house and a bank account—but enjoys hardly any meaningful communication with the other married partner. That's the Lonely-in-Love.

I recently had breakfast with one of America's leading businessmen. He told me of a long and happy marriage that had fallen on troublesome times. In part, he said, the problem was caused by the constant traveling demanded by his business and stewardship responsibilities. He felt his wife was unhappy with his frequent absences from home, and yet it was not a lifestyle he could easily withdraw from. Eventually he talked it out with her, and he was surprised at her response. "It's not the fact that you travel that creates my problem," she said. "It's the fact that when you get back home you're still traveling."

This isn't an unusual example. In fact it's a common illustration of what is happening on every corner of the continent. Millions of married people endure incredible loneliness even though they live in the same house. They have physical proximity but emotional distance.

Inez Spence, author of *Coping with Loneliness*, refers to wives suffering in this way as "work widows." But I want to stress that the Lonely-in-Love can be either husband or wife. Nor does the loneliness stem purely from the prolonged absence of one partner. Spence cites the case of a couple from a Northern city. The husband came home only on weekends. They had no children, but even though the wife missed her husband and looked forward to his return at the end of the week, she refused to brood over her seclusion. She overcame her shyness in order to develop a full social life, and she took up Spanish and music. In other words, partners of a marriage with heavy work commitments do not need to end up among the Lonely-in-Love.

Of course this kind of loneliness does not last forever. If a wife sees marriage as the cause of her loneliness, the pressure will be to either improve the marriage or end it. If it cannot be improved, in all likelihood she will gradually change from the Lonely-in-Love to the Outsider, and the failure of the personal relationship will be followed by the failure of the legal, financial, and parental ties that previously held the couple together.

The initial phase of breakdown that produces the Lonely-in-Love is less common in other kinds of relationships. It rarely occurs in friendship, for example, because the ties are only personal: Once two friends have fallen out there is nothing else left; no legal ratification of the breakdown is necessary, and they are free to drift apart. Of course the Lonely-in-Love may occasionally be a child who is provided for by his parents but is otherwise completely ignored.

4. *The Top Dog.* Two employees are sweeping the stockroom as the boss leaves work one day. They're complaining about the economic situation. One says to the other, "This inflation's killing me. I don't know how I'm going to pay the grocery bill on Friday night." Just then the boss drives by in a Cadillac. The man who's speaking watches him go and says, "Boy, that boss sure is lucky! See that big Cadillac he's got? There's nothing wrong with me that 5000 bucks wouldn't take care of!"

What they don't know is that the boss in the Cadillac is a nervous wreck. He's in a cash crisis, but he can't tell anyone. He knows that if the bank finds out what a precarious position he's in he may have his loans called in. And if that happens he's finished. He drives home with nothing on his mind but his financial problem. He has to live with it because he's the Top Dog.

It's a fact that leadership brings a certain kind of loneliness—the loneliness of responsibility. That's on top of all the strains imposed by the executive lifestyle. One man told me recently that to succeed in today's commercial world the entrepreneur needs the nerves of a riverboat gambler. I can believe it. But businessmen aren't the only victims. If anything, politicians have it even worse. So, in a way, do stars and celebrities, though their loneliness has more to do with being recognizable than responsible.

But the Top Dog isn't always playing to 30,000 fans in a football stadium or leading a board meeting of some vast corporation. He's likely to be standing in your church pulpit next Sunday.

You can take it from me as an insider that clergymen experience pangs of indescribable loneliness. The pastor has no pastor. He is on call 24 hours a day. He is under pressure to pay more visits than a country doctor, produce more public addresses than a full-time lecturer, supervise a financial program larger than many small businesses, and preside over more disputes than the head of a labor union. On top of that he is required to take marriage services, and has the dubious pleasure of conducting funerals and being the bearer of heart-breaking news to the victims of disaster. And often it's just as tough for his wife, as Mrs. John Lavender, wife of a West Coast minister, made clear in her book entitled *They Cry, Too*.

The Top Dog may have a loneliness different in character from the other four lonely people I'm writing about, but it's no less harrowing. In fact it can be more so. If you are the Top Dog, this book is for you too.

5. *The Ugly Duckling.* It's likely that any kind of lonely person will eventually become an Ugly Duckling.

The Sandgrain and the Outsider are particularly prone to develop in this direction. The change occurs in the way the person thinks about himself. The Ugly Duckling doesn't only feel isolated, or lost in the crowd, or rejected. He feels positively inadequate.

In many cases the sense of inadequacy focuses on some perceived imperfection in the individual concerned. He becomes enslaved by certain features of his body or personality that appear to block the path to self-actualization. A 15-year-old high school boy, for example, may feel inferior about standing at only four-feet-eleven and suffering from an asthmatic condition. High school isn't the easiest place to forget peculiarities like that. His classmates call him "Shorty." He can't participate in sports because of his asthma. It wounds him deeply to see the girl he likes (who is at least six inches taller than he is) ogling at some six-foot sportsman who looks like Harrison Ford.

Asthma and puniness are two personal idiosyncrasies taken from a list of almost infinite length. A person can feel self-conscious over practically anything. With women it's often being overweight, having lines on the face, or having legs of the wrong shape. Men fret over losing their hair or being physically weak or shy. Kind friends will point out to the sufferer that his problem is more noticeable to him than to other people. But once a person has become the Ugly Duckling the reality behind the perception often ceases to matter. A nose that is only slightly larger than average appears to be absolutely enormous. An inability to sustain conversation (which might in more charitable moments be passed off as natural reticence) is taken instead as incontrovertible evidence that the person is a social cripple.

Unfortunately, the feeling of inadequacy tends to be reinforced by the media. The television, film, and advertising industries continually bombard us with stereotypes to which the "successful" human being is assumed to conform. I won't go into details. Five minutes in front of your TV set will supply all the evidence you need. The point is that we are confronted every day with the yawning gap between real life and life as the media implies it should be lived. And because the latter characteristically requires a big income, the majority of viewers are left with the feeling that they are in most respects substandard. So far as the advertisers are concerned that is all to the good, since if you feel bad about yourself you're more likely to buy something to improve your image. It's not far from the truth to say that producing a nation of Ugly Ducklings—people lonely through a sense of inadequacy—is a principal aim of the advertising industry. Loneliness doesn't pay, but it certainly buys!

The supreme farce of this media image-building is demonstrated in the blandness of the images. For example, almost any American would be flattered if you called him an "individualist." Individualism is an image which the media persistently encourages us to develop. The fact that we are being encouraged to think of ourselves as "individualists" while at the same time achieving a uniformity of appearance and outlook comparable with a string of bologna sausages is an irony that somehow escapes our notice! True individualism is less common today than it was in the age of the settlers. We talk about individualism to obscure the fact that we are not as individualistic as we would like other people to think we are. We like to seem individualists because that is the popular image of the moment—what will make us acceptable to our peers. But behind the image, Americans (and probably many people in other Western countries) are hiding more Ugly Ducklings than they would care to admit.

3

Beyond the Ugly Duckling

Which of those five lonely people are you? You may feel you are more than one—the Outsider as well as the Top Dog, for example. But I will be surprised if you haven't thought hard about putting yourself in the fifth category, the Ugly Duckling, because what characterizes the Ugly Duckling is the most natural human reaction to loneliness. It's called *self-doubt*.

If you are the Ugly Duckling, you are at a critical point in your life, for two reasons.

One, which I will return to later, is simply that this is the time to act. You're like the triple jumper who has reached the end of his run and has to take his first leap. The second reason is that once you have begun to experience self-doubt as a result of your loneliness, the nature of the problem changes. Loneliness is never a pleasant experience. But beyond the Ugly Duckling stage, loneliness acts like a disease and starts to develop complications. We might divide them into two types—the *psychological* and the *spiritual*.

Understanding these two types is crucial if you are going to win over loneliness.

The Psychological Complications: Disintegration

It is impossible to live with a personal idiosyncrasy—overweight, shyness, or whatever—without turning your attention inward. You feel there is something "wrong" with you. You may be justified in reaching that conclusion, or you may not. That doesn't matter. The very fact that you have reached the conclusion is evidence of the change in your thinking, and in time this will start to alter your behavior.

This reorientation toward introspection happens all too easily. In America, do-it-yourself psychiatry could almost be

33

described as a national pastime; a wide range of books, thera-
pies, and self-help groups are available to help us with it. A
fundamentalist Christian may find the pressure even greater,
because fundamentalism is naturally inclined to be introspective. For every sermon calling unbelievers to salvation
there is another calling the faithful to scrutinize their con-
sciences and rededicate themselves to the pursuit of holiness.
The desire for personal sanctification is good, of course—
how could it not be? But the weakness of fundamentalism lies
in giving it disproportionate attention, so that the believer is
forever on guard for his soul as if it were a picnic in danger of
an invasion of ants.

Don't misunderstand me—I don't mean to draw an equa-
tion between searching your conscience and the gloomy contemplation of failure. Clearly the first is a positive exercise,
and the second negative. But the person who is accustomed
to looking inward in prayer will find it easy to look inward
again when he is lonely. And this negative introspection
leads to four further problems.

1. *Ineffectiveness.* It only makes sense that the more energy
you devote to introspection, the less you will have for God,
for other people, and for the work that God is calling you to.
That in itself is enough to make introspection a dubious
hobby. But it doesn't stop there. The harder you look at your
supposed inadequacy, the more you undermine your confidence. You start driving with the brakes on, not just when
you're cornering but when you should be flying down the
straight road. If you are lonely you will know what I'm talking
about here. Loneliness is enervating. It saps your drive and
motivation. It takes your eyes off your goals. And there's
nothing strange about that—it is the direct result of gazing
inward.

Also, can I remind you that ineffectiveness isn't your own
private problem? It lets down those who are depending on
you. Like Cain, we all have a God-given responsibility to
support others, to be "our brother's keeper." By forcing us to
self-doubt, loneliness sabotages this support. We begin to

think less about other people's troubles than we do about our own. We get self-obsessed. Imagine a board meeting where the company secretary is so busy fretting over his personal problems that he never takes the minutes! Yet the poet George Herbert describes Christians as "secretaries of God's praise." How can we praise God properly, and help others to do the same, when we ourselves are downcast by loneliness? The answer is, of course, we can't. Loneliness makes us ineffective.

2. *Illness.* There is ample evidence to indicate that all states of anxiety, introspective loneliness included, induce sickness through stress. Among the direct physical results of loneliness are headaches, high blood pressure, strokes, psychasthenia and gastrointestinal problems. Further secondary effects will arise if loneliness disrupts our sleep patterns and eating habits. And there's worse news than that. In the book *Executive Health* (published by *Business Week*), Philip Goldberg, president of the International Institute of Stress, writes that disappointment, loneliness, and unhappiness are factors correlating with a high incidence of cancer.

An article in *Time* magazine on the same topic lays the blame squarely at the feet of loneliness ("Loneliness can Kill You," September 5, 1977):

> Health studies have long shown that single, widowed and divorced people are far likelier prey to disease than married folk. Some examples: the coronary death rate among widows between 25 and 34 is five times that of married women in the same age group. At all ages, the divorced are twice as likely as the married to develop lung cancer or suffer a stroke. Among divorced white males, cirrhosis of the liver is seven times more common, and tuberculosis ten times more common.
>
> Why should it be so? To psychologist James J. Lynch, 38, author of a new book, *The Broken Heart: The Medical Consequences of Loneliness*, the answer is

obvious: loneliness kills. Says he: "Loneliness is not only pushing our culture to the breaking point, it is pushing our physical health to the breaking point. . . . Simply put, there is a biological basis for our need to form human relationships. If we fail to fulfill that need, our health is in peril."

3. *Idealization*. There is some merit in being an idealist, but none in idealizing situations that we should be assessing in the cold light of reason. Life isn't a breeze. When God said to Adam, "In the sweat of thy face shalt thou eat bread," He was laying down a principle that holds good for all human endeavor. If we want to achieve something, we had better be prepared to work for it. And we had also better be prepared for "Murphy's Law," by whose inexorable decree matters left to themselves will always turn out to our disadvantage! Such is the nature of the world we live in.

The blissful newlyweds should not be surprised when their marriage sees its first argument.

The entrepreneur should not be taken unawares when his rival tries to steal a copyright.

The new pastor should not feel mistreated when his new charge turns out to be a hotbed of unforeseen problems.

No one, and certainly no politician, should be discouraged to find that he has enemies.

I could extend the list indefinitely. The point is that anyone with any experience of real life knows he won't get his own way all the time. After the first few knocks he adjusts his expectations to reality, and if that doesn't stop him from getting hurt, at least it saves him from disappointment. He doesn't like arguing with his wife, but he knows that marriage has its trying moments, so he doesn't let arguments discourage him. Both he and his wife are only human, after all. Soon the argument blows over, and he finds afterward that they're none the worse for having weathered the storm. Perhaps they're even a little wiser.

In contrast, the lonely person is conscious of his or her own isolation and has far higher expectations of other people.

The young couple that is lonely for fellowship with other Christian couples in a new city will often have an idealized view of the church they join. They expect to walk in one Sunday morning and immediately be included in the social circle, as if faith alone entitled them to the privileges of personal friendship. When they are not invited to someone's house for coffee right away, they are highly critical of the church and doubly lonely.

A divorced woman, new to this particular experience of loneliness, can easily have inflated expectations of a date. Because she needs friends and has so few, she gives the occasion an importance that is out of all proportion to reality. Consequently she may suffer disappointment when the man seems not to have looked forward to it quite as much as she did, and feels let down when the evening, which might be perfectly pleasant in its own right, fails to fulfill her expectations. Instead of getting a boost from it, she just feels more lonely.

In the area of work, a lonely person can give too much importance to the approval that others give to his achievements. He convinces himself that his colleagues or clients will be overwhelmed by the new concept that he has come up with, and will congratulate him on his ingenuity. If they don't—or even if they give him the kind of moderate praise that is usual on such occasions—he takes it as a personal snub. He has, in effect, made his acceptance totally dependent on his professional performance. The idea that he could make friends anyway, whatever his work record, doesn't occur to him. The only way he can think of to counter his loneliness is to prove that he's a genius—a tough assignment indeed!

Unrealistic expectations lead to disappointment and deepen loneliness. But also, as is clear from the three examples given above, a lonely person's idealizing puts pressure on the people around him. This is a dangerous side effect of loneliness. Often, if others show any interest in him at all, a lonely person will expect them to give him priority and to be understanding, sensitive, and perpetually close by. In short, he makes conditions so intolerable for others that any potential for friendship is quickly killed off. He becomes known not only as a lonely person but as a demanding one—somebody to be pitied and avoided.

Needless to say, that does nothing to relieve his loneliness!

4. *Introversion.* Often the final stage of loneliness is an almost-complete social introversion.

This may be a state of clinical depression in which the sufferer has neither the will nor the ability to break out of loneliness. But it may also be a deliberate, aggressive response which calls necessity a virtue and tries to stave off emotional pain by pretending that isolation is better than friendship. After all, a rock feels no pain.

But when the rock is a human being it *does* feel pain. There's no escaping it. That's why the end of the loneliness road is such a desolate place. It is particularly desolate for elderly people in cultures that are increasingly geared to the young. In Britain, for example, the old extended family has largely disappeared and the care of the elderly is now the responsibility of the state. But even though the state can pay for health care, it has no cure for loneliness. Thousands of elderly people die lonely every year. For many of them loneliness is a contributory cause of death.

You don't have to be old for loneliness to kill you. In elderly people loneliness hastens death by depriving the victim of the will to live, but for increasing numbers of young people in America and other Western countries the link is more direct: Loneliness pushes them to suicide.

The Spiritual Complications: Sin

I'm not going to pull any punches here. Loneliness that has passed beyond the Ugly Duckling stage is almost certain to be a sin.

Coming so soon after describing the desperation of the lonely, this may sound a bit harsh. The last news that a lonely, self-doubting person wants to hear is that he is sinful as well as inadequate! Because of this, let me say again that the experience of loneliness comes to us first as a pain. There's nothing sinful about being on your own or missing the company of those you love. That far you share your experience of loneliness not just with me but with all Christians and with Jesus Christ Himself.

But pain of any kind brings us face-to-face with temptation. Temptation is something that every committed Christian has to deal with. Jesus "was in all points tempted like as we are, yet without sin" (Hebrews 4:15). The power to resist temptation in any area of life—the same power that Jesus had—is one of our privileges as children of God. We are not helpless when tempted; God has given us the capability of self-determination. Within the limits of our gifts and our environment, we determine what we become. We determine whether we will be influenced by a certain desire, a certain point of view, or a certain personal pain. Sometimes the pressure to bend will seem enormous, almost irresistible. But God never leaves us unattended. As Paul wrote to the Corinthians:

> There hath no temptation taken you but such as is common to man; but God is faithful, who will not suffer you to be tempted above that ye are able, but will with the temptation also make a way of escape, that ye may be able to bear it (1 Corinthians 10:13).

Remember the last time someone was spiteful to you? Like loneliness, that experience is a pain. And when it happened two possibilities confronted you—either saying yes to your own feelings of hurt and revenge (and therefore no to God) or else saying no to those feelings and yes to the way of forgiveness that Jesus spoke of in the Sermon on the Mount: "Whosoever shall smite thee on thy right cheek, turn to him the other also" (Matthew 5:39).

In essence, the temptation offered to us by loneliness is no different from that. When you suffer the pain of loneliness the choice pops up in front of you, and you must decide. You cannot avoid deciding. Either you say no to your natural inclinations and yes to God or else you say yes to your natural inclinations and no to God. The second choice—which, by the way, you may well make without even noticing it—moves you from suffering loneliness as a pain to indulging it as a sin.

Briefly, let me explain what is involved in that yes and no.

In the case of loneliness, "natural inclinations" means three interrelated types of behavior. If you like, you can use them as a test, right now while you're reading, because if your loneliness has given rise to them you have certainly made that all-important transition. Just one word of warning: Be sure to be honest. There's absolutely nothing to be gained by cheating, because the only one you'll fool is yourself.

1. *Self-centeredness.* You don't have to go far to find someone being selfish. But selfishness and loneliness are often strongly linked. Take the following example.

A young man has recently gotten married. He adores his wife and wants her to be proud of him. They have nothing, but he is determined to be a success, so he works and works, rising rapidly up the ladder of achievement. Promotion after promotion propels him steadily upward. Soon he is able to buy a lovely home in suburbia and to provide his wife with her own car. The children, now in their teens, can be placed in a private school. He and his wife start to be seen with the right people and belong to the right clubs.

But instead of rejoicing over his achievements, his wife begins to complain because he travels so much and works so hard. She whines that she would rather have less and be able to lead a normal life with a husband who is at home when the family needs him.

He's stung by this. He can hardly believe his ears! "Less" has a more specific meaning for him than it does for her. "Less" means going without a second car, putting the children back into public schools, canceling club memberships, eliminating expensive vacations, and going without the luxuries they have now come to regard as basic necessities (central heating and air-conditioning, big color TV sets, and athletic equipment for the children). Worst of all, "less" means moving to a less desirable part of the city and dropping a few rungs down the social ladder.

He knows his wife wouldn't accept any of these changes, and yet he's being criticized for pursuing the very job that makes them possible. He feels unappreciated, abandoned, even betrayed—not just by his wife, but by the children too. They have started to be distant with him. Like their mother, they're treating him as though he owed them the time he cannot give. They don't seem to understand why he can't come to every football game or school activity. They don't seem to make the connection between his absence from the house and the automobiles they drive, the expensive clothes they wear, and the money that helps them be accepted by their peers.

He feels isolated from his family. His wife and children feel isolated from him. Loneliness intensifies and leads to resentment, anger, and reproach. And it's because the family members have responded to loneliness with self-centeredness instead of with love and understanding.

2. *Discontent.* A lonely person will almost always feel discontent with the state of his life.

He perceives a clear association between his loneliness and the mediocrity he experiences in his work, his recreation, and his family life. Paul's parting advice to the Philippians—"Rejoice in the Lord always, and again I say rejoice" (Philippians 4:4) is totally lost on him. He cannot rejoice because fate seems to have made his situation unhappy. As a result, his conversation will carry an undercurrent of complaint. He will have no time for other people's woes because he is always airing his own.

Besides being an outright rejection of the commands given in the New Testament to love and rejoice, such behavior actually intensifies the problem. Nobody likes a complainer. He will tend to be ostracized, thereby producing a downward spiral in which complaining becomes the cause as well as the expression of his loneliness.

3. *Self-pity.* Though self-centeredness and discontent are sinful consequences of loneliness, neither is central to an understanding of loneliness and sin. But self-pity is. In fact it's the key to the whole question.

There must have been something of the Top Dog in Elijah when, after being called on to represent God in the contest on Mount Carmel, he retreated miserably into the desert. He had played his part as God's champion against the prophets of Baal, but with Jezebel breathing threats down his neck the responsibility suddenly felt too much:

> When he saw that, he arose and went for his life, and came to Beersheba, which belongeth to Judah, and left his servant there. But he himself went a day's journey into the wilderness, and came and sat down under a juniper tree; and he requested for himself that he might die, and said, "It is enough; now, O Lord, take away my life, for I am not better than my fathers. . . . I have been very jealous for the Lord God of hosts, for the children of Israel have forsaken thy covenant, thrown down thine altars, and slain thy prophets with the sword; and I, even I only, am left; and they seek my life, to take it away" (1 Kings 19:3,4,10).

Clearly Elijah's distress arises from loneliness—he is, he feels, God's last man in a nation of apostates. Not only that, but God has just made him commit the worst possible offense by killing 400 prophets of the official religion.

Notice how Elijah shows some classic psychological complications of loneliness. The fact that he is in this state at all seems to arise from his own unrealistic expectations. Did he really think the whole job would be a cinch, that Jezebel would let him get away with killing her prophets? Apparently so, for the news of her displeasure seems to have come as a complete surprise to him. Consequently he is now on the run, feeling isolated and completely ineffective. He thinks obsessively about his limitation and loneliness until they have blocked out the rest of his vision. Yet being "better than his fathers" had never been an issue before now; and as for being alone, even Elijah must have known that Baal worship wasn't universally accepted in Israel. Actually, God had reserved not one or two faithful men but *seven thousand*! Yet Elijah's loneliness blinded him to that fact. He had become so turned in on his own misery that he even wanted to die.

The keynote of Elijah's condition is *self-pity*. The little speech that he makes to God purports to be a summary of the facts, but it actually boils down to a plea for sympathy. In effect he is saying, "See how faithfully I have obeyed You? Now just look where it's gotten me!" He's doing what any self-pitying individual tends to do—handing out two propositions to the world and expecting the world to underwrite them. One says, "I've done everything right and so I'm not to blame for the present state of affairs." The other says, "Because I am a victim it is your duty to pity me."

Self-pity is a pathetic and unattractive trait. A self-pitying person has abdicated responsibility for his own life. He's on emotional welfare. His situation, of course, is completely sterile—nothing will ever come of it. But it is also unnecessary. If I refused to pay my bills on the grounds that I was bankrupt, I would be lying. The impediment would be rooted not in my financial state but in my *will*. And so it is with self-pity. When Elijah had finished talking, God didn't simper over him and say, "You poor creature, what a terrible bind you're in!" What Elijah saw as the cause of his problem God simply ignored: "The Lord said unto him, 'Go, return on thy way to the wilderness of Damascus' " (1 Kings 19:15). In other words, "Quit jawing and get back to work!"

The lonely person who pities himself is declaring a sort of social bankruptcy that has no real existence. There is a solution to loneliness—that's my reason for writing this book and yours for reading it. For a person to say, "I'm lonely, so feel sorry for me" is as ridiculous as having your bank manager ask you to lend him a dime. He has all he needs. And so does the lonely person, *if he will only accept it.*

Here is the crux of the solution: The answer to loneliness may be obtained simply by saying yes to God. It is the Bible's answer, and it is explained in detail in this book. So you are presented with a choice. On the one hand is the opportunity of winning over loneliness. On the other hand is the temptation of sinking into self-pity. You can't have both. They're as impossible to mix as oil and water. Say yes to God and you will be breaking out of your inertia just as Elijah did in setting out for Damascus. But choose self-pity and you'll be seeking sympathy instead of a solution. You'll be throwing aside God's answer to loneliness and hungrily demanding commiseration. Self-pity won't act, won't help itself, won't listen to advice. When you pity yourself you give God a resounding no.

That's why self-pity is a sin. In fact, saying no to God is almost a definition of sin. Eve said it when she picked the forbidden fruit in Eden, and human beings have been saying it incessantly ever since. In every case there is the possibility of saying yes. Eve could have obeyed God's command and let the fruit alone. Think back over the last 24 hours and I'm sure you'll be able to think of half a dozen times that you've faced a similar choice. The temptation to self-pity in loneliness is exactly the same.

I stress the issues of sin and decision because winning over loneliness cannot be done without recognizing the nature of the problem, or giving your mastery of it 100 percent commitment. Later I want to deal with the answer that God has provided to loneliness, but first I want to look at some non-answers. Being in the throes of self-pity won't stop you from looking for ways out, so it's worth being able to spot those so-called solutions to loneliness that will lead you, like Elijah's retreat to the wilderness, up a blind alley.

4

How Not to Win Over Loneliness

What do you do when you've got a toothache?

My guess is that you pick up the phone and make an appointment with your dentist. But suppose that when you phone, your dentist refuses to give you an appointment. "No need to see me," he says. "Just do 50 push-ups every morning, and if that doesn't take your mind off the pain, try chewing gum or seeing a good movie."

Would you take his advice? Of course not. If you've got a pain, and you want to get rid of it, you want some really effective treatment. There are countless options open to the person with a toothache. Many of these, including doing push-ups and seeing movies, may bring some benefit of their own, but they won't relieve the person of his pain.

Toothache and loneliness may not seem to have much in common, but they are both pains, one mental and the other physical. Also, they both stimulate a desire to escape. That is one of the basic functions of pain. If I did not get a stinging sensation when I strained a tendon I might cause myself a serious injury. Pain hurts me for my own good.

But of course I can only escape a pain if I know what causes it. Finding the cause can be hard with a physical pain—dentists have been known to pull the wrong tooth!—but it's usually even harder when the pain is mental. For example, what is the fundamental cause of pain in marital breakdown or depression? In all likelihood there will be many causes, some of them unique to the person or persons involved. This makes analysis difficult. It also means that the treatment will be more involved than taking a trip to the dentist.

What about the mental pain of loneliness?

Well, the fact that causes are hard to identify obviously puts the sufferer at a disadvantage. But there is another factor at work here too, a kind of diagnostic red herring, because anyone who comes to loneliness via self-doubt—that is, as the Ugly Duckling—already has a firm notion of what is making him lonely. It's the spotty complexion, the bad breath, the fat, the nervousness, the isolation caused by fame or responsibility. The Ugly Duckling's most pressing problem, after all, is his ugliness!

Yet as I hinted at the end of the last chapter, ugliness of whatever variety is not the decisive cause of loneliness. Though it may underlie the initial experience of loneliness as a pain, the prison door to the "loneliness syndrome" is locked shut by the sufferer's personality, not his circumstances. Until he recognizes this fact, the lonely person is like a prisoner busily trying to open the door with keys that do not fit the lock.

These false solutions, or misfit keys, generally fall into one of two groups. The lonely person, remember, works from the assumption that loneliness arises from his unacceptability. On that premise he has two options. One is to come to terms with his inadequacy, and turn from his frustrating attempt to make friends to another, easier kind of fulfillment. The other option is to make his unacceptability more acceptable—to make the Ugly Duckling look more like a swan. I call these options the Blockout and the Facelift.

The Blockout

One kind of blockout is *travel*.

I'm not talking about annual vacations. For the ordinary man or woman in the street, two weeks of sunbathing in Honolulu is a welcome break from the daily routine and a chance to make new friends. But the lonely traveler won't often be found on a tropical beach. There is too much there to remind him of his loneliness and not enough to stimulate his imagination. He tends to prefer strange and distant places where his mind will be occupied continually with new challenges and new experiences. If he visits crowded centers he will go for ones populated by foreigners. In Venice or Bombay his contemplation of the wonders of human culture is less likely to be disturbed by intruders who speak his own language. On a cruise (he often takes cruises because he can remain anonymous and quiet and still go somewhere) the crew will respect him as a recluse. They will think of him as eccentric rather than lonely, which suits him well because no one likes to admit to loneliness. The combination of this esteem and his regular diet of novelty will (he hopes) make an adequate substitute for friendship.

Sooner or later, though, most lonely travelers—and I have seen many of them—return home bored and disconsolate. There simply aren't enough new experiences in the world for them to survive. At this point many of them turn to another kind of blockout—*spending*. They may have turned to it during their journeys around the world, or maybe they tried spending first and then went on to travel afterward. It doesn't make much difference, because both attempt to counter loneliness in the same way. Travel goes in search of novelty in faraway places, while spending brings it into the living room. Either way, novelty can satisfy for only so long. In the end the string of redecorations, expensive cars and jewelry, Ming vases, and Warhol originals will tangle into the familiar dull knot, and the lonely person will be forced once again to confront his loneliness.

Travel and big spending, of course, are privileges open only to the comparatively wealthy. Most people have to be content with less extravagant solutions. But a popular kind of blockout available at the lower end of the market is probably more effective than either of the first two. It's called *television*.

The secret of TV's appeal to the lonely person is its ability to produce a sense of inclusion in society. That can be a benefit. For an elderly person who suffers real and painful isolation, television can fill a yawning social gap. For my son Johnny, who was confined to a wheelchair and unable to converse in a normal way, it gave access to entertainment and information that he would otherwise have gone without. In situations like that, TV can be a benefit.

But of course I cannot give it my unreserved endorsement. For one thing, watching TV is a passive exercise. No effort is required, no creative thinking called for. It may provide a useful service for those limited by age or illness, but toward the healthy and mobile it can act as a form of disablement. The lonely person is too easily addicted to it, and so loses the drive, the willingness to struggle, the discipline essential for dynamic living. I believe that the trademark for success is the sweatband—and nobody sweats watching TV. Compulsive viewing deprives the lonely person of the skills required to carry on a decent conversation or engage in any productive enterprise. In the end it deprives him of the means by which he can feel good about himself. It turns him into a full-time receiver.

That is a danger inherent in TV viewing regardless of program content. Human beings are designed to relate to one another, not to cathode ray tubes. Documentaries may have more educational value than situation comedies, but neither engages the viewer in a real relationship. At the end of the evening he goes to bed with only the illusion of having been in company.

But the fact that television in general has this illusion-building quality does not make the question of program content unimportant. Some illusions are better than others, and many of them are downright deplorable. How much useful advice on the formation of sound relationships will the lonely person get from the average soap opera? And what kind of values will he pick up while watching movies with crude language and unwholesome themes? If he switches channels to a talk show he won't do much better. Talk shows deal with real people, but they also give the featured celebrity a platform to speak in authoritative tones on subjects in which he is a total incompetent. A man may be able to lay his opponent out cold in three rounds, but does this talent make his views on rearing children worth hearing? And what about the film star beginning her fifth marriage—is she the person best qualified to tell the nation about love and family life? I hope not!

The fact is that besides substituting TV for normal social relationships, the compulsive viewer exposes himself to a barrage of unedifying, misguided, and sometimes plainly harmful opinions. The only possible effect of all this is confusion and increased loneliness. I have never met anyone I considered emotionally healthy who spent hours every day watching soaps, sick movies, and negative talk shows. I'll be surprised if I ever do.

Television also encourages *overeating*, which as a kind of blockout deserves a mention in its own right. The fight for first place in the lonely person's affections can often be between the TV and the refrigerator. Like television, eating is a way of relieving boredom, and so it is common for the day spent in unwanted solitude to be punctuated by "snack attacks," especially if the lonely person is by nature an introvert.

For people who are not satisfied by TV and whose value systems allow it, there are two more extreme forms of blockout—*alcohol* and *drugs*. Both do television's job—of sinking the user in illusion—but both do it more efficiently. Alcohol has the advantages of being legal, relatively cheap, and (at least until the victim hits skid row) socially acceptable. But like heroin, it's an addictive drug, and addictive drugs of any kind, though they seem to offer an escape from loneliness, will in fact savagely compound it. There aren't many people who want a wino for a friend! Nor is there any real friendship to be found in the company of other drinkers, addicts, and pushers. Alcohol and drugs are really just options of self-destruction.

The final type of blockout I have left until last—not because it is the most dangerous but because in Western countries it is so seldom recognized. The word was coined by Dr. Wayne Oates in 1971—*workaholism*.

Because we are conditioned by the Protestant work ethic to regard work as inherently good, I want to approach my definition of workaholism carefully. Let me do it first by comparing two men.

One is Sir Bruce Small of Australia, who started life as a Salvation Army "brat." He began to repair bicycles in his teens, went into bicycle sales, and then manufactured his own design, the Malvern Star. In the 1920's and 30's he sponsored Hubert "Oppy" Opperman, probably the most durable cycling champion the world has ever seen. In 1960 he retired at the age of 65, with 30,000 employees and the largest bicycle empire in Australia.

Did I say "retired"? He moved to the coast of Queensland and began developing what is now known as the Gold Coast— probably the most famous resort area in the continent. At 76 he ran for parliament and won. As an octogenarian he didn't walk—he trotted. I have actually seen him run to his car! His schedule, at a time of life when most people are in decline, would have killed a man one-third his age. He made himself available. His telephone number wasn't unlisted, so anyone who wanted to could contact him directly. But for all that, he is far from being a compulsive worker. He knows how to pace himself, when to stop, which way to relax.

Compare him with Dick Vermeil, formerly coach of the Philadelphia Eagles. Like Sir Bruce, Vermeil has worked hard. The team knew him as an intense man, so committed to his job that he kept a cot in his office to keep him from wasting time on the trip home. He used it often. And he was successful—he took the Eagles to the playoffs and the Superbowl. But he couldn't keep it up. In 1975, at the age of 46, he turned down an offer from the Atlanta Falcons (which incidentally included part ownership and total control of the organization), and instead opted to retire. The reason? The work had burned him out. He was a brilliant coach, but his almost-fanatical devotion to his work had demanded the total sacrifice of his social and family life. His private happiness, he decided in the end, was a price he was no longer willing to pay.

Sir Bruce Small and Dick Vermeil exemplify the difference between hard work and workaholism. Superficially it's a difference that's hard to see, for both men have achieved success, and both have done it by industry, commitment, and vision. I would be the first to admit that success comes no other way. But just as winning a Grand Prix demands more of a driver than putting his foot on the accelerator pedal, so the achievement of success ultimately depends on a person's ability to control work. Streaking into the lead in the first lap is no good if you're going to run out of gas before the end of the race, or if you come off the circuit taking a curve too fast. The driver must control the car—not the other way around.

Uncontrolled work spills over from office hours into time that, for the well-being of the workaholic as well as those around him, should be given to other concerns and activities. The connection between workaholism and loneliness is clear, for in many cases workaholism develops through a person's inability to cope with social and family life. This saddles him with a feeling of isolation. Of course the various other types of blockout are available to him. But the workaholic is too restless to watch TV and too respectable to resort to alcohol or drugs. So he works. From his perspective this is a near-perfect solution. Work is self-justifying: His colleagues would criticize him for taking time off, but when he voluntarily gives up his evenings for the sake of the company they stand in awe. Not only that, but work gives him an impressive excuse for avoiding painful company, and yields enough success to protect him from the suspicion—which never leaves him—that he is really pathetic and inadequate.

The catch with workaholism is its cost. Like drugs, it has the side effect of increasing a person's social isolation. And this means that (also like drugs) workaholism needs to be taken in bigger and bigger doses to remain effective. But of course the human body can't cope with overdoses of work any more than it can withstand prolonged alcohol abuse. Sooner or later emotional or physical breakdown occurs— usually both. And at the end the workaholic is no nearer overcoming the nagging self-doubt that for so long chained him to his desk. Gail Sheehy, author of *The Pathfinders*, puts it succinctly:

In the process of subordinating everything else to the drive to enter the winner's circle—the expectation that then insecurity will vanish and one will be loved and admired and never again humiliated or made to feel dependent—the gulf of loneliness grows wider and wider. . . .

The Bible provides ample stimulus to hard work, but it never advocates workaholism.

One definition of the workaholic is: "A person who can't stand Sundays." As was pointed out by one child in a compilation by Marshall and Hample called *God Is a Good Friend to Have*, "God made a lot of days so He wouldn't try to do everything at once." If God observed a time of rest, and even wrote the principle of rest and relaxation into His commandments, there is no excuse for Christians who try to cover up loneliness with excess labor. John Wesley traveled a quarter-million miles on horseback, preached an average of three times daily for over 60 years, and wrote 371 publications. Nevertheless he observed his quiet time every day. Yet despite long hours in solitude, his diaries show no trace of loneliness.

That's *real* work!

The Facelift

There is a range of cosmetic surgery available to the Ugly Duckling. The object, of course, is always the same—to convince other people that he's a swan.

The easiest method is to stay far enough away that nobody notices the difference. In practical terms this means keeping social contact on an entirely superficial level—never allowing conversation to rise above triviality, never risking emotional entanglement, never allowing oneself to care or be cared for. This method works very well—provided that you don't mind coming across as utterly bland and uninteresting, and spending time with other people who come across to you the same way. People using this method may give the impression that their social life is like one long ride on a roller coaster, but that is the shared myth which makes the whole illusion tolerable. Superficial relationships are, almost by definition, unrewarding relationships. You are in no danger of being "found out," but by the same token you are unable to gain from your social life any real antidote to loneliness.

Once you get close enough to other people for deeper relationships to be possible, the cosmetic surgery starts in earnest. But no sooner have you dispensed with the old, unacceptable face when another problem confronts you: What do you put in its place?

One solution is to dig around in the closet until you find something from the past. If you don't like the way you are now, it's tempting to pretend that you're still the way you used to be—or, more likely, the way you *think* you used to be, for the past always has a tendency to don its best hat and pose as "the good old days," even if at the time it wasn't much different from the present. But no matter how astounding our past accomplishments, God has not given us the power to resurrect them. When we try to, the result is often sad and ridiculous. I remember as a young man seeing a lady of 65 or so trying desperately to sing as she had done in her twenties. It was meant to impress people, to counter her loneliness. But she would have done better to accept her decline with grace, because she only succeeded in making everyone embarrassed for her. It reminded me of that sad moment in the story of Samson, when Delilah, having betrayed his trust in her by cutting off his hair, rouses him in the middle of the night:

> And she said, "The Philistines be upon thee, Samson." And he awoke out of his sleep and said, "I will go out as at other times before, and shake myself." And he knew not that the Lord was departed from him (Judges 16:20).

The fact that occasions like this arouse pathos rather than admiration is proof enough that our past will never meet the needs of our present. And that leaves the lonely person with a choice of three further kinds of facelift.

If he can't look to his past, any "new face" inspired by his own personality will have to come from the way he is now— and that means it will have to incorporate the fact of his loneliness. He can do this by projecting loneliness positively or negatively. The positive projection presents him as a loner, a person who gets along fine on his own and doesn't need anyone else. A lonely lady will sometimes let on that she is lonely, but she will add that she can cope with it because "that's the kind of person I am." This is slightly less aggressive, but it is still a positive projection of loneliness, presenting it as something warranting respect and admiration. In contrast, the negative projection asks loneliness to be pitied. The person who uses it is cashing in on his predicament in much the same way as a beggar who draws attention to his crippled foot. He is admitting he's different, but he is also using that difference to substantiate his claim to special attention. In the beggar's case the attention may be demanded in the form of cash; with the lonely person it is more likely to come as lavish helpings of time and sympathy. Having someone say "You poor thing . . ." is better than having no one at all.

Both these projections, of course, ultimately have the effect of driving other people away. Somebody who tells you his loneliness is an asset is—or appears to be—making it clear that he's not interested in friendship. On the other hand, a person for whom friendship and commiseration are broadly synonymous terms isn't likely to keep his friends for very long!

So much for finding a "new face" somewhere in your own past or present.

But this leaves a third option: seeking inspiration in other people. One beneficial spin-off from this option is that the lonely person may inadvertently discover the biblical answer to loneliness. However, he usually doesn't. Much more likely he will try one of the cheap panaceas available in the form of paperbacks, radio and TV talks, and articles in women's magazines. Only if he is very lucky will the solutions suggested by an "expert" be of any use to him. Sometimes they are disastrous even to their creator! Not long ago I saw a Hollywood star holding forth on a network talk show about methods of coping with loneliness. Listening to him you would have thought him the world's foremost authority on the subject. But only a few days later I noticed newspaper headlines loudly announcing his death. The reason? Suicide provoked by loneliness.

I'm not telling you it's wrong to follow another person's advice or example. I've already said that as a teenager I got a lot of help from the book my mother gave me about cultivating friendship with the right people. But that's precisely the point—they have to be the *right* people. A person's willingness to appear on TV or write in a magazine is no proof that his thinking is sound. He may be an imbecile, and a charlatan to boot. The warm, deep waters of human need are all too often infested with sharks!

So let me emphasize again that there is only one answer to loneliness. An expert who knows his job may be able to give you some useful tips, and a trustworthy acquaintance may set a good example for you, but you will ultimately win over loneliness *by seeking God*. Everything else will fail you in the end. As the psalmist said, "My flesh and my heart faileth, but God is the strength of my heart and my portion forever" (Psalm 73:26).

5

God's Promise to the Lonely

God's promise to the lonely person starts with one of the Bible's loneliest people. As it happens, he was a Top Dog. But that doesn't matter, for what God taught him would apply equally well to the Sandgrain, the Outsider, the Lonely-in-Love, or the Ugly Duckling. His name was Joshua.

Joshua took over the leadership of Israel at a critical point in the nation's history. After wandering for 40 years in the wilderness and defeating Og and Sihon, the people of Israel were just about to cross the Jordan River and enter the Promised Land. It wasn't the time for confidence to falter. Yet at this precise moment, Moses, the man who had led them out of Egypt, announced that the Lord had not permitted him to cross the river. The psychological effect of that is easy to imagine. Moses was the man who had confronted Pharaoh, divided the Red Sea, brought water from the rocks of the desert, and met God at Mount Sinai. By any reckoning that was a hard act to follow!

Consider how Joshua must have felt in receiving the mantle of leadership from Moses. Was he honored to serve God this way? Perhaps, but he was also aware of the sheer enormity of the task before him. Once he had gotten the Israelites over the Jordan (and that wasn't going to be a cinch) he was faced with the prospect of conducting an armed invasion. Trudging through the wilderness was one thing, but taking on the tribes of Canaan in warfare was quite another. On top of this, though the Israelites accepted Moses' choice of Joshua as a successor, in the position of leadership Joshua was still untried. He still had to show he was up to the job.

At first everything went his way. He impressed his authority on the Reubenites, the Gadites, and the half-tribe of Manasseh (all of whom had elected to stay on the east bank of the

Jordan) by persuading them to play their part in the forth-coming campaign. He then sent spies into Jericho, the nearest Canaanite city. They returned with good news: The Israelites' reputation had gone before them, and "even all the inhabitants of the country do faint because of us" (Joshua 2:24). Joshua then broke camp from Shittim and proceeded to the Jordan, his own "Red Sea." On the Lord's instructions he sent the priests down first, bearing the ark of the covenant, and for the second time in Israel's history seemingly impassable waters split open before them. "On that day the Lord magnified Joshua in the sight of all Israel; and they feared him, as they feared Moses, all the days of his life" (Joshua 4:14).

The loneliness of leadership is always sweetened by success. The real challenge comes in failure—and it was a challenge that Joshua was soon to meet. After the fall of Jericho he approved a plan to take the city of Ai with a small, expeditionary force of only 3000 men. For reasons he was not yet aware of, the attempt was to prove a disaster:

> The men of Ai smote of them about thirty and six men; for they chased them from before the gate even unto Shebarim, and smote them in the going down; wherefore the hearts of the people melted, and became as water (Joshua 7:5).

For their new leader this was a dangerous setback. It seemed to prove that Israel was vulnerable in her isolation among the tribes of Canaan. After all, if a small city like Ai could put them to flight, what about the larger ones? Fear spread through the camp. Joshua, who up till now had ridden on the crest of the wave, felt himself sliding down into the trough. He almost lost his nerve:

> Joshua tore his clothes and fell to the earth upon his face before the ark of the Lord until the eventide, he and the elders of Israel, and put dust upon their heads.
>
> And Joshua said, "Alas, O Lord God, wherefore hast thou at all brought this people over the Jordan,

to deliver us into the hand of the Amorites, to destroy us? Would to God we had been content, and dwelt on the other side of Jordan! O Lord, what shall I say, when Israel turneth their backs before their enemies! For the Canaanites and all the inhabitants of the land shall hear of it, and shall environ us round, and cut off our name from the earth; and what wilt thou do unto thy great name?" (Joshua 7:6-9).

His sense of isolation comes across loud and clear. Not just as leader of the people, but as an individual, he was starting to feel abandoned. And his mind had gotten jammed up with the projected consequences of that abandonment. He started to fantasize. In fact he was the lonely Top Dog reacting badly in a crisis, obsessed with the thought that the whole pile might be collapsing under him. That fear of being engulfed by circumstances comes in a special way to the Top Dog, but it is a fear shared by all lonely people when they look at the future. It is like standing in a hall of crooked mirrors where everything is distorted and blown up out of its proper size. Joshua could think of nothing better to do than prostrate himself.

But God had other ideas:

> The Lord said unto Joshua, "Get thee up; wherefore liest thou thus upon thy face?" (Joshua 7:10).

Having dragged the uncharacteristically weak-kneed Joshua back onto his feet, the Lord set about instructing him. He did it in two ways. First, He made it clear that the failure which Joshua connected with his own sense of loneliness was in fact a separate issue, with its own causes and its own resolution: "Israel hath sinned . . . for they have even taken of the accursed thing, and have also stolen, and dissembled also, and they have put it even among their own stuff. Therefore the children of Israel could not stand before their enemies" (Joshua 7:11,12). Joshua's responsibility as leader was to root out the offenders—who had disobeyed God's specific command not to plunder the ruins of Jericho—and to put Israel back in a right relationship with God.

Second, God reminded Joshua of a special commitment He had made to him as leader of the people. Here it comes in the context of a reassurance about Ai: "The Lord said unto Joshua, 'Fear not, neither be thou dismayed; take all the people of war with thee, and arise, go up to Ai. See, I have given into thy hand the king of Ai, and his people, and his city, and his land' " (Joshua 8:1). But the principle itself God had laid down in the words of Moses just before Joshua took over:

> Be strong and of good courage; fear not, nor be afraid of them; for the Lord thy God, he it is that doth go with thee; he will not fail thee nor forsake thee (Deuteronomy 31:6).

The promise is repeated a few verses later:

> The Lord, he it is that doth go before thee; he will be with thee, he will not fail thee neither forsake thee; fear not, neither be dismayed (Deuteronomy 31:8).

Finally the promise appears again, directly from God, as Joshua takes up his new responsibilities: "I will be with thee; I will not fail thee nor forsake thee" (Joshua 1:5).

God could hardly have rubbed it in any harder. He is dealing with the very heart of Joshua's drive and motivation. He assures Joshua that He is constantly at his side, and that He won't leave him or let him down. He asks Joshua to let that fact sink into his consciousness. In the heat of God's presence, Joshua is told, his fears will evaporate. Knowing that God is beside him, he can take the initiative with fresh courage and confidence.

In other words, in Joshua's personal crisis over the defeat at Ai, events acted only as a trigger. The real problem was that

Joshua had lost sight of God's promise. All of a sudden he had been looking at the situation the way it *seemed to be* and not the way it *really was*. If he had taken to heart God's promise never to fail or forsake him, he wouldn't have wasted an afternoon lying on the ground with earth on his head. He would have put loneliness in its place and gotten on with the job.

Joshua Today

"Fine," you may say. "That's all very well for Joshua. But the fact that some Old Testament leader got a promise from God doesn't make life any easier for me!"

But wait a minute. The same phrase that God used when He addressed Joshua also crops up in the New Testament, in the letter to the Hebrews. In the list of instructions near the end of the book the writer says this:

> Let your conversation be without covetousness, and be content with such things as ye have; for he hath said, "I will never leave thee nor forsake thee." So that we may boldly say, "The Lord is my helper, and I will not fear what man shall do unto me" (Hebrews 13:5,6).

This passage is a powerful affirmation of God's caring love. But note carefully how the writer reaches his conclusion. "You do not need to be anxious for material goods," he says, "because God has promised to be with you." He quotes directly from Joshua 1:5. (He couldn't have got the phrase from anywhere else because Joshua is the only person to whom the promise was given in that form.) So what is he implying? Simply this: *The full weight of reassurance and strength contained in that personal promise which God made to Joshua now applies to all His children.* To put it another way, whoever you are and whatever "Ai" you face, God looks on you as a Joshua. It doesn't matter what kind of lonely person you are. When God says, "Get up; why do you lie upon your face?" He means *you*. When God says, "I will be with you; I will not fail you or forsake you," He means *you*.

That's why I want you to remember that verse. It is the foundation of God's answer to your loneliness and the key to your victory over it. So why don't you write it out right now, in big bold letters, and put it in some prominent place where you will be able to see and read it several times a day? Make it soak into you. Say it to yourself until the meaning goes all the way from your head to your toes: I WILL BE WITH YOU; I WILL NOT FAIL YOU OR FORSAKE YOU!

God with Us

Hebrews isn't the only book to attest to the fact of God's personal presence in the lives of believers; it is fundamental to the entire teaching of the New Testament.

Men like Joshua were exceptional under the Old Covenant. Though God's glory went with the Israelites in the tabernacle constructed under the leadership of Moses, He had not promised to be "with" every member of His chosen people in such a personal and individual sense. In later centuries, when the early zeal of the Israelite invaders had given way to complacency and apostasy, and finally brought on the exile, the prophets often looked forward to a time when God's presence would be established in a fuller and more permanent way:

> I will make a covenant of peace with them; it shall be an everlasting covenant with them; and I will place them, and multiply them, and will set my sanctuary in the midst of them for evermore. My tabernacle also shall be with them; yea, I will be their God, and they shall be my people (Ezekiel 37:26,27).

This vision of Emmanuel—"God with us"—was fulfilled more literally than even the prophets suspected. In the famous words of John: "The Word was made flesh and dwelt among us (and we beheld his glory, the glory of the only begotten of the Father), full of grace and truth" (John 1:14).

There was to be no return to the old concept of the divine presence. The tabernacle in which God finally appeared was not made with hands. It was the body of a human being; Jesus Christ, fully God and fully man.

For God to have exchanged the splendor of the temple for incarnation might at first seem a poor move. In the days before television and newspapers, the power of one individual to be "with" a large number of people was severely limited. A relatively small number actually followed Jesus around on His travels, and of these only 12 were selected as close companions. In addition to this, the human body is notoriously vulnerable. It gets tired. It can be hurt. It can be killed.

These two factors—limitation and vulnerability—seemed to figure large in the disciples' fears for Jesus. The journey to Jerusalem, where Jesus was effectively a wanted man, promised a swift foreclosure of His whole mission. But Jesus didn't see it that way. The death He allowed Himself to endure was a necessary step in the program of redemption, just as the "death" of the seed sown in the autumn is necessary to the growth of next year's crop. Destroy this temple, and in three days God would raise it up. And after raising it He would be with His people in a way never before dreamed of:

> Now I go my way to him that sent me; and none of you asketh me, "Whither goest thou?" But because I have said these things unto you, sorrow hath filled your heart. Nevertheless I tell you the truth: It is expedient for you that I go away; for if I go not away, the Comforter will not come unto you; but if I depart, I will send him unto you (John 16:5-7).

The sending of the Comforter (*parakletos*, literally "one called alongside") marked the birth of the Christian church. As Peter said on that first Pentecost: "This is that which is spoken by the prophet Joel: 'And it shall come to pass in the last days,' saith God, 'I will pour out of my Spirit upon all flesh' " (Acts 2:16,17). No longer did God withhold Himself from mankind. From that moment His supernatural presence in the Person of the Spirit was given to any who repented of sin and named the name of Christ. In fact that very act of repentance, says Paul, draws us into a unique association with God that may be described not just as the Spirit coming to the believer but as the believer dwelling in God:

> If ye then be risen with Christ . . . set your affection on things above, not on things on the earth. For ye are dead, and your life is hid with Christ in God. When Christ, who is our life, shall appear, then shall ye also appear with him in glory (Colossians 3:1-4).

You might say that the Christian is about as near to God as he or she can get without actually going to glory. Our life is "hid with Christ in God," and meanwhile we enjoy the constant, supportive presence of the Comforter as we go about our business here on earth. Did I hear someone say he was lonely? Read those passages over again! What possible room can we have for loneliness when God has given Himself to us, first in Christ and then in the Holy Spirit? Answer: none at all. As Christians we enjoy the unique privilege of friendship with God every moment. Even when we suffer the most appalling isolation, through bereavement or responsibility or whatever, God honors His promise to be near us: "I will be with you; I will not fail you or forsake you."

Nor is the promise of God's companionship reserved for a few pious souls who perform great works or have great spiritual experiences. It is for *every Christian*, with no strings attached. If you're a Christian, it's for you. God is with you right now. The Comforter is at your side, just as Jesus said He would be. "Ah," you reply, "but the problem is that I don't *feel* as if He is." Well, then, forget your feelings! We're not talking feelings here; we're talking facts. You may feel cold, but if the temperature outside is 90 degrees in the shade your feelings aren't telling you anything about the weather. Winning over loneliness doesn't start with feelings. It begins with the central and incontrovertible fact that God is with you.

You're Not Alone!

Build your awareness of God's promise, because you can't start winning over loneliness from anywhere else.

But at the same time know that God has given you a kind of free bonus to help you on your way. You see, Christianity was never meant to be a private matter. When Peter preached his first sermon on the day of Pentecost, and the membership of the church exploded from a hundred or so to over 3000, the apostles didn't say a blessing over the new converts and then send them home. The church became a community, "continuing daily with one accord in the temple, and breaking bread from house to house" (Acts 2:46). And that, in one form or another, was the way Christianity spread over the Roman Empire. Most of the epistles in the New Testament are addressed to churches, but even the ones to single Christians—like Titus and Timothy—deal with church matters. Christian faith may have begun with the commitment of individual hearts, but after that it was assumed to find its expression in the life of the Christian community.

This "collective" aspect of our relationship with God has strong doctrinal roots. Listen to Paul writing to the Galatians about their new status as members of God's family:

> When the fulness of time was come, God sent forth his Son, made of a woman, made under the law, to redeem them that were under the law, that we might receive the adoption of sons. And because ye are sons, God hath sent forth the Spirit of his Son into your hearts, crying "Abba, Father" (Galatians 4:4-6).

Here is Paul again, this time picking up the themes of the Christian's closeness to God and the role of the Holy Spirit:

> He [Christ] is our peace, who . . . came and preached peace to you who were afar off and to those that were nigh. For through him we both have

access by one Spirit unto the Father. Now therefore ye are no more strangers and foreigners, but fellow citizens with the saints, and of the household of God, and are built upon the foundation of the apostles and prophets, Jesus Christ himself being the chief cornerstone . . . in whom ye also are built together for a habitation of God through the Holy Spirit (Ephesians 2:14,17-20,22).

We are adopted sons in God's family, fellow citizens in God's kingdom, bricks in a temple occupied by God Himself. The metaphors are unanimous: Besides receiving the promise of God's friendship, the Christian exists in a community of men and women committed to the same goal as he is. He travels in a pilgrim band. He is not alone.

Just being a member of a church, however, does not guarantee friendship. Every parent knows that children don't have to be together long before they argue. Bricks meant for the temple wall may not have the most accommodating shapes. That's why so much space in the epistles is devoted to matters of church order, encouraging Christians to love one another as Christ commanded them to. I emphasize "as Christ commanded" because there is a lot of talk today about the *feeling* of love. The feeling is unimportant; what counts is *action*. I can talk all I want about my feelings of love for famine victims in the Third World, but until I translate that love into *action* (for example, by sending money or praying), I'm talking through my hat. Feelings don't save lives.

Feelings don't relieve loneliness, either. Saying you love your brothers and sisters in Christ can be a way of keeping your distance from them. You can sound off about love every Sunday and actually be Lonely-in-Love, because the external signs of church fellowship are hiding a lack of real substance.

Dr. George W. Truett once had a visit from a lonely man he had known all his life. The man had come to announce his decision to leave the church. "You're such a good friend," he said, "that even though I don't believe in God, I felt it was courteous to come and tell you before I went."

Dr. Truett nodded. "Okay," he replied. "But will you do me one last favor before you go? There is a dear man from our congregation in the hospital. Would you go and read 1 Peter to him?"

Glad to be let off so lightly, the man agreed and went straight to the hospital. A few hours later he came back, shaken. As requested, he had read the epistle; but this simple expression of love changed him profoundly. Suddenly love had become action, not words, and he had found himself leading the sick man in prayer. In doing a favor for an old friend, he had come out of the morass of unbelief.

The church ought to function as a resource for the lonely person. It is part of his or her heritage as a Christian to be a member of the family of God. But the fact that the church community isn't always as open and caring as it should be underlines the point that God, not the church, is the only sure answer to loneliness. Nobody's perfect. So don't rely on the love of other Christians to solve your personal loneliness. They're meant as a help, but *only* as a help; if you come to depend on them they may let you down. Your victory over loneliness can be built on one foundation only—the promise God made to Joshua, which still stands true for you and for every Christian: I WILL BE WITH YOU; I WILL NOT FAIL YOU OR FORSAKE YOU.

Rely on that, and you will win over loneliness!

6

Two Essential Secrets

Now we come to the heart of God's solution to loneliness.

As we have found out already, loneliness will not be solved either by compensating for it—the *blockout*—or by revamping your image—the *facelift*. These approaches may divert your attention for a while, but because they fail to address the real causes of loneliness, in the end they can only compound it. The true answer to loneliness comes through the promises of God, and when confronted by that divine answer, loneliness is put to flight.

It doesn't matter what kind of lonely person you are. The Sandgrain, the Outsider, the Lonely-in-Love, and the Ugly Duckling will all lose their loneliness. And the Top Dog, though he cannot escape the isolating effect of his work, will be enabled to cope with that isolation and to eradicate all other forms of loneliness from his life.

But here's the catch.

If you want this revolution to happen to you, you'll have to apply yourself. God's solution isn't like a crash diet that's over in a couple of weeks. It is nothing less than a complete reorientation of your life. I will draw a simple analogy with the construction industry. A developer who wants to turn part of the inner-city slums into a brand new housing estate doesn't begin by putting new wallpaper in old houses. What's already there is built in the wrong way and for the wrong purpose. The whole plot needs to be leveled before anything useful can be done with it. So the developer starts not by decorating, nor by repairing existing structures, but by tearing down old and outmoded buildings to make way for the new.

In tackling loneliness, the most essential task often *seems* to be the mending of relationships with other people. Much popular therapy available in books and magazines concentrates on this challenge. Learn how to relate, they say, and you will discover the key to overcoming loneliness. But the problem is that while mending relationships is the object of winning over loneliness, it is not the place to begin. Wallpapering is a waste of time if the plaster is crumbling and the brickwork is unsound!

So don't be fooled with simplistic solutions. You'll get what you're prepared to work for. If you're satisfied to live in a damp and drafty building with nothing changed except the wallpaper, that's your choice. It won't take much effort to put the wallpaper up, but by the same token you won't gain much satisfaction because after a couple of months in a leaky house the mold will reappear and you'll be back where you started. Of course we can extend the analogy and allow you to do a bit more than change the wallpaper. You could replace a few tiles on the roof and treat the dry rot in the floorboards. But why be content with half-measures when you can get a whole new house?

God, you see, is like a master developer who has plans to rebuild your life according to His perfect specifications. Allow Him to guide you as to tackle the "slum" of loneliness, and your life will undergo a dramatic change. But be prepared to follow *His* plans and not your own. Only He can do the job properly. And remember that the mending of relationships, the "decorating," is the final stage of the process. There are other matters you must attend to first in order to make that final stage really effective. So follow the plan from the beginning.

I have already asked you to remember the verse from Joshua on which God's solution to loneliness is based. If you can recall that verse now, you're already on your way to winning over loneliness. (If you can't, go back and learn it!) To help you forward from here, I have summarized God's plan in a simple three-point formula. It outlines the task ahead of you in the order in which you must tackle it. Commit the formula to memory. It is God's blueprint for your victory over loneliness:

Get right with GOD
Get right with YOURSELF
Get right with OTHERS

You'll notice that the three points of the formula correspond to the next three section headings in this book. Each of those sections goes into more detail on the action you should take in order to accomplish that particular stage of the task. But before you turn the next few pages, I want to emphasize two important principles—*Discipline* and *Dependence*. I haven't put these in the formula, but I guarantee that you'll need them.

Imagine yourself standing in an international airport, about to begin a business trip. You will probably have two pieces of luggage with you: an attache case containing all the papers and materials you need for your meetings, and a suitcase carrying your pajamas, toothbrush, and extra shirt. Both cases are essential if the trip is going to be a success. You can't go to a meeting without your notes, but you wouldn't want to turn up with a dirty collar, either.

Discipline and *Dependence* are like that—essentials in the business of tackling loneliness. They're needed because the job of winning over loneliness is in a sense a joint venture between you and God, and this demands that you have a good working relationship with both parties. *Discipline* governs your attitude toward yourself; *Dependence* governs your attitude toward God.

Discipline

I am a great admirer of Michelangelo, and I am in good company when I refer to him as a genius. But had I said this to his face he would not have regarded it as a compliment. Hearing it used of him one day, he fumed, "Twenty hours a day for 14 years I worked, and you call it *genius*?" Thomas Edison took much the same view. He always used to say that his inventions were 2 percent inspiration and 98 percent perspiration!

Both men had mastered the art of discipline, and both saw it as the cornerstone of their achievement. A little thought reveals their approach to be absolutely sound. No athlete gets to the Olympics by sitting around with his feet up. One said recently that he practiced six to eight hours a day for more than six years to reach his present standard of excellence.

It's the same in other fields of endeavor.

The pianist Paderewski labored at the keyboard eight hours every day.

George Bernard Shaw wrote for ten long years before a publisher would accept his work, and Ernest Hemingway revised his prizewinning novel *The Old Man and the Sea* no less than 46 times!

Have you ever seen the name Otis on an elevator? Next time you do, remember that this man failed as a mechanic on three occasions before he developed his now-famous invention.

And did you know that Mary Martin was once told by an acknowledged authority in show business that she had no talent for singing? She put the discouragement aside and eventually made it to the top. The price? Discipline!

People sometimes seek to evade discipline by saying they have faith. Now I am the last person to disparage faith. Faith in the promises of God lies at the heart of what I am saying in this book. But as James pointed out with respect to salvation, "faith without works is dead" (James 2:20). Faith needs to be validated by action. The man with great faith is not the one who leaves everything to God—that comes perilously close to laziness—but the one who works in everything *with* God. To have faith is to employ God's power. Imagine a miner who said to his boss, "Yes, the explosives are there in the store-room, but I'm just waiting for them to go out and blast the granite!" This would be nonsense. It's true that explosives are vital to the production of coal or iron ore or whatever, but they won't do a bit of good if nobody places them and sets the charges. So it is with faith: God never does for us what we are able to do for ourselves.

This principle is clearly taught in Scripture. Jesus raised Lazarus from the dead, but he didn't make the stone roll away or loosen the graveclothes. It took the disciplined effort of a group of men who rolled the stone back to make faith effective. "Show me thy faith without thy works," says James, "and I will show thee my faith by my works" (James 2:18).

In every part of our lives it is our responsibility to use discipline to "show" our faith. The finest opera star starts only with potential. No amount of faith will turn that potential into excellence—only the hard work of discipline will do that. It's exactly the same with the emotions. Loneliness isn't going to vanish just because you pray about it. God isn't going to pick it up like a heavy suitcase and carry it for you, just like that. Nor can you expect to get rid of it by receiving large doses of love from other people. Would you rely on God, or your friends, to make you stick to a diet? Of course not! They might be able to give you motivation and encouragement, but if you can't discipline yourself, they won't be able to do it for you.

Discipline is vital for withstanding all kinds of challenges— not just loneliness. You need a basic strength in your emotional life so that unexpected and massive changes—like the death of a loved one, the betrayal of a friend, or the bankruptcy of a business—won't sabotage your joy and sense of well-being. Your emotions need to be in good health in order to take the jolts and disappointments of life, just as your body needs to be rested and properly fed in order to cope with the sometimes-exhausting demands made on it by long hours, sudden crises, and sleepless nights. Human life can be a rough ride. Every Christian has faced times of hardship and of storms that almost capsized the ship. There may be a few storms in store for you as you fight against loneliness. Remember: *In such moments discipline is indispensable.* In fact I tell you flatly that you won't win over loneliness without it.

What if you are one of the most poorly disciplined and disorganized people around? Never mind. Hasn't God promised to give you all you need? Pray for discipline, and day-by-day God will supply it to you.

It surprises me how seldom Christians do that. I've listened to many prayers in my lifetime. I have heard requests made to the Lord by old and young, sick and healthy, happy and the distressed. There have been prayers of gratitude and thanksgiving, prayers for missionaries in foreign lands, prayers pleading for the salvation of family members, for money to pay bills, for the healing of loved ones. We rightfully pray for wisdom, strength, patience, and submissiveness. But think—how often have you heard anyone pray for self-discipline?

Maybe the real problem is that we don't really want it.

Discipline makes demands on our time and commitments. It can be compared to achieving physical fitness. There's no 11-minute-a-day panacea for loneliness. To get results you need to take on a tough regime that will leave some long-unused muscles aching. Sometimes you may feel weary in spirit and be tempted to give up the new lifestyle in order to go back to the simpler misery of being lonely.

But take heart. Getting fit emotionally may be grueling, but at the same time it's rewarding, and often fun. There will be payoffs. You will start to feel better about yourself. You'll have a continually spring-fresh attitude to buoy you through the day. You won't hate the sound of your alarm clock in the morning, nor will you be frittering your nights away with futile games when you should be sound asleep.

But once again, remember that knowing the formula, knowing God's promise, will not in itself help you win over loneliness. *Truth must be applied and principles acted on.* So stop and consider now, before you begin, whether you're willing to pay the price. If you're not, quit reading this book right now and take it back for a refund.

Dependence

In the summer of 1935, as an 11-year-old boy, I was on vacation with relatives in Grand Rapids, Michigan. One day my cousin Alex and I were walking up Burton Avenue with groceries that he had picked up for his mother.

Suddenly three big fellows in a pickup truck pulled over to the curb. "Hey, Haddad!" they yelled. "Get yourself and that blankety-blank Hebrew, Wop, Dago cousin of yours out of here before we mop up the gutter with you!"

I cringed. Bitter experience at school had taught me that taunts like that usually heralded a beating. But as I was bracing myself it suddenly occurred to me that my 15-year-old cousin Alex was the wrestling champion in the 175-pound division. He had biceps like cannonballs and pectoral muscles like marble slabs.

I pulled back my shoulders and said, "You're not going to let them get away with that, are you?"

But Alex was looking straight ahead, not breaking his step.

"Well, John, you know what the Bible says: 'Whosoever shall smite thee on thy right cheek, turn to him the other also.' "

That perplexed me. I had never remembered Alex being quite that spiritual before. But I didn't argue, and Alex continued to ignore the abuse. At last we reached the house. But just as we opened the gate to the picket fence, Alex stopped and handed me the groceries.

"John, give these to Mom. I forgot something. Tell her I'll be back in a few minutes."

I knew what he'd forgotten. Quietly I placed the groceries inside the front door and tailed Alex back down Burton toward Seymour Square, to an ice-cream parlor where the young folks gathered. He figured they would be there. They were.

I arrived just in time, and stood in the shadows between two buildings. The three boys were out of the pickup now. Alex took on the biggest one first, hitting him so hard he went out like a light. He dazed the second with another blow. When he turned around the third was fleeing in terror. A smile crept over my face, and I brushed the palms of my hands together, thinking, "Anyone else?"

Looking back on it today, neither Alex nor I would condone what he did that afternoon. But I'm not concerned at the moment about the ethics of retaliating to abuse. The point I want to make is that having Alex around made me act in a different way. His presence transformed me from an abject coward into a confident young man. Alex was my helper, my protector, and his bravery made me brave.

Loneliness can be as terrifying a problem as those bullies were to me when I was a youngster. But it is not a problem you face alone. I've said already that God is with you in the Person of the Holy Spirit. Well, this is where His presence counts. He can defeat your loneliness and transform your attitude to one of joy and victory, just as Alex did for me. Would you feel lonely if Jesus were with you in His physical body? Of course you wouldn't. And you have something even better than that, because the Comforter that Jesus promised to send His disciples in John 16 lives not just *with* us but *in* us. That's why Jesus said, "It is expedient [or 'advantageous'] for you that I go away." Why advantageous? "If I go not away, the Comforter [or 'Helper'] will not come unto you" (John 16:7).

Jesus was saying that God's spiritual presence in the Holy Spirit would be of more use to the disciples than His own bodily presence. At the time they found that statement hard to believe, but they soon realized He was right. Paul says in Romans that "the Spirit also helpeth our infirmities" (Romans 8:26). This means that He helps us deal with our loneliness. The verb translated "helpeth" means literally "to receive with, alongside." It suggests a picture of one man standing alongside another, helping him lift a heavy load. It's not that the Spirit lifts the load for us—we still have to exercise discipline and use our powers to the full. But He will assist us, give us strength, and ensure that no load comes our way that we cannot handle (cf. 1 Corinthians 10:13).

There is no qualification needed to get the help of the Spirit. If you are a lonely person who has turned to God for help, that same power which God used to raise Jesus from the dead will be applied to your loneliness. Paul calls it "the exceeding greatness of his power to us who believe" (Ephesians 1:19). Try to imagine loneliness coexisting with resurrection power. Unthinkable!

But let me give a word of warning. The power of God is not to be trifled with. Loneliness is the opposite of all that the Spirit aims to do in your life. The fruit of the Spirit is love, joy, and peace, but loneliness distorts love, devastates joy, and destroys peace. It is inward-turning and self-destructive, robbing both you and others around you of the potential blessings of your life. To turn to that weakness voluntarily is what moves loneliness from the area of pain to that of sin. So make a conscious effort to cooperate with the Spirit on a day-to-day, moment-by-moment basis. You don't have to be perfect (none of us is that!), but you do have to keep up a firm determination to continue the fight.

Getting Help

The difficulty which people have in depending on their heavenly Helper is an understandable one—they can't see Him. In this respect, for Jesus to have gone away seems anything but advantageous! So what are we to do when we are tempted to give in to loneliness, and we have no visible evidence of the Spirit at our side?

The answer, of course, is to have faith. Faith is, after all, the evidence of things not seen. Furthermore, belief is what opens the way to God's deliverance. God never operates in the area of unbelief. Just as Jesus could not do many miracles in Capernaum because of the people's unbelief, so the Holy Spirit is unable to work in your life if you doubt His ability or His willingness. Feelings are not the issue here. You don't have to "feel" God's presence and not many people do. Just take it seriously when God says He will help you. If He says it, it's a fact!

"But," you ask, "how do I receive this faith?"

First, don't be halfhearted. Give God free rein in every department of your life. He must have the keys to every room in your heart. If you don't trust Him with those keys, you're missing out on faith.

Second, dwell upon the trustworthiness of the Benefactor. After all, you've trusted God for your salvation, and you trust your friends and colleagues as a matter of course. Why then is it so much trouble to believe it when God says He is always with you? Isn't He absolutely trustworthy? Faith is acting on the thing you say you believe as though it were so. You say you believe that God will provide and the Holy Spirit will help. Now act on it.

Third, live in the Scriptures. "Faith cometh by hearing, and hearing by the word of God" (Romans 10:17). Nothing will produce faith as effectively as the Word. Read it. Even as you doubt, keep reading. As you read, say, "This is for me. God loves me. He cannot lie. He wants to meet my every need. Loneliness grieves Him. He wants to deliver me. The Holy Spirit wrote this Book. He, living in my heart, wants to speak to my need through His Book."

Fourth, keep daily records. I find that when I pause at the end of the day to reflect on what God has done. I am astounded. If I jump into bed, conscious of my exhaustion but unmindful of the specific blessings of that day, I build up an attitude that says, "Boy, living for Christ sure is a drag!" So ask yourself what God has done for you, and let that memory strengthen your faith.

Remember—faith gives you access to the power of the Spirit, and it is dependence on the power of the Spirit, allied with firm self-discipline, that you need in order to win over loneliness. If you're ready to accept these two vital principles and use them to the full in your quest to overcome loneliness, you'll succeed.

Part 2

GET RIGHT WITH GOD

7

The Thanksgiving Habit

Fifty years ago my father announced ten messages he intended to preach on forthcoming Sunday nights. One of the titles I remember above all the rest. It was: "The Worst Sin."

What sin could it be? For weeks the congregation speculated. Some said it was unbelief. Others said it was the unpardonable sin of blasphemy against the Holy Spirit. Still others said it was suicide.

But they were all wrong. When the day came to preach on "The Worst Sin" my father mounted the pulpit and calmly announced it as *ingratitude*. Ingratitude? Yes, he explained, because it is the most basic of sins. He went on to show how ingratitude preceded even unbelief in the rebellion of Adam and Eve. Had they been grateful for God's provision, they would not have rebelled against their divine Benefactor.

Dad piled up one piece of evidence upon another. I recall especially his quotation of the passage in Romans where Paul says, "When they knew God, they glorified him not as God, neither were thankful, but became vain in their imaginations, and their foolish heart was darkened. Professing themselves to be wise, they became fools" (Romans 1:21,22).

"Neither were thankful." When he read those words a chill passed over the congregation as young and old alike realized the dire consequences of ingratitude. Dad was absolutely right. Ingratitude sums up man's rejection of God. And because of that, it is the foul source of all the poisoned streams of wickedness. It is also the cause of man's spiritual loneliness, that isolation from the love of God that is beyond the reach of any therapy except the cross.

But if ingratitude drives a wedge between man and his Creator, the converse is also true: Thanksgiving draws Him closer. Therefore it is hardly surprising that gratitude is the hallmark of the Spirit-filled life. Study the life of Jesus and notice how often He gave thanks. Read some of the epistles and see how this divinely ordained habit was passed down to Paul. "In everything give thanks," he wrote to the Thessalonians, "for this is the will of God in Christ Jesus concerning you" (1 Thessalonians 5:18). And to the Colossians: "Whatsoever ye do in word or deed, do all in the name of the Lord Jesus, giving thanks to God and the Father by him" (Colossians 3:17).

Developing a habit of thanksgiving is the best way to start getting right with God. Giving thanks directs your attention away from yourself and toward the Lord. It cultivates an awareness of unity with the One you are thanking, and it demonstrates respect. Yet it doesn't require the mastery of any complicated technique—on the contrary, nothing could be simpler. And it can be inspired by the ordinary events of life. Anything, from sunshine to a smile, can prompt you to give thanks, and once you are giving thanks all those feelings of isolation and loneliness begin to be starved off.

Of course life isn't all sunshine and smiles. But with a little practice you can make thanksgiving work for you in the bad times as well as the good. Turn to the Psalms. The psalmist knew what suffering was about. In Psalm 35 David opens with a plea for God to deliver him from his enemies:

> Without cause have they hid for me their net in a pit, which without cause they have digged for my soul (Psalm 35:7).

Yet a few lines later he gives thanks, and the tone of the psalm begins to change from complaint to joy in God's victory:

> I will give thee thanks in the great congregation; I will praise thee among much people . . . and my tongue shall speak of thy righteousness and of thy praise all the day long (Psalm 35:18,28).

Thanksgiving always undermines negative thoughts. Pessimism, fear, loneliness, and worry are helpless before it. The reason is that thanksgiving not only gets us right with God but also bounces back to give us a true perspective on our problems. As Paul said, we have much to give thanks for because we are "abounding in all things." That is the truth. Even if you are the loneliest Christian in the world, you "abound in all things," and that "all things" includes peace, joy, and fulfillment. Does this mean that it's dishonest to give thanks while you feel lonely? The answer is no, and I'll tell you why. First, the blessings—of peace and joy and so on—are already yours, in spite of the fact that you're not making use of them. Second, thanksgiving helps you to realize these blessings in your own experience.

I call this "the Smith Effect."

The Smith Effect

In my first little pastorate I would stand at the door to shake hands with people as they departed during the postlude. One of the ladies always passed by with a pained expression. Oh, how miserable she looked! She had a face like an accident waiting to happen.

"How are you today, Mrs. Smith?" I would ask.

"Very poorly, pastor. Pray for me."

I am extremely sensitive to other people's moods. If I don't take steps to protect myself, I find myself feeling the same way they do. Consequently this ten-second exchange with Mrs. Smith usually left me feeling terrible.

One day I said to my wife, "I believe that Mrs. Smith is the ugliest woman I have ever seen."

"Nonsense," my wife replied. "Why, she is basically a beautiful person."

"Well, if she is, the beauty is so basic I can't find it!"

"Maybe you ought to pay her a visit. She may have some serious problems."

So I went to visit her. Now I'm used to every kind of home, and I certainly don't expect a person to keep a house looking like a museum. But Mrs. Smith's living room pushed me to the limit. She had clothes lying on every item of furniture. I returned home to tell my wife that Mrs. Smith's house was as much a problem as her countenance.

As time went on Mrs. Smith became more and more of a problem for me. I knew my attitude was wrong, and I felt guilty at not pleasing the Lord. Something had to be done. The question was: what?

One Sunday morning on our way to church my wife must have seen that I was preoccupied because she turned to me and said, "John Edmund Haggai . . ."

I knew that when she used my full name she meant business. I raised an eyebrow.

". . . I don't know what you've got in mind, but you're up to some mischief, and I am going to pray that you won't do it."

"You're too late," I replied. "I've been praying about this for two weeks. I have a head start on you!"

When Mrs. Smith came out of the church that morning, I was ready for her. I put iron in my backbone and cracked my face in a Pepsodent smile that showed all 32. Grabbing her hand and pumping it vigorously, I said, "Mrs. Smith! You are looking *so* much better today. I know you must be feeling better!"

God forgive me—it wasn't really a lie, but more a statement of faith, faith being the substance of things *hoped for*, the evidence of things *not seen*!

Mrs. Smith batted her eyes. For a moment she seemed stunned, but then a faint smile wreathed her face and she said, "Thank you, pastor. I believe I am feeling a little better."

I let her take back her hand, and she walked out the front door. In a matter of weeks she was not only feeling better but looking better.

I am tempted to say that if the Smith Effect can work on Mrs. Smith it can work on anyone! Certainly I know many people who have benefited from it greatly. One of them is Aletha Bergman, an 83-year-old widow living in a little village in Georgia. In her youth she was one of the Christian world's most effective women leaders. She was on the staff of the late Robert G. Lee, who built the congregation of the Bellevue

Baptist Church of Memphis from a few hundred people to nine thousand.

I have visited Aletha Bergman. She admitted freely that her health was so poor she could have died at any moment. Yet she showed not the slightest trace of loneliness. She didn't pine for the past or complain about the present. The way she dressed, the way she had fixed up her little apartment, and the way she sparkled and bubbled put flight to any suspicion of loneliness. I'm not sure she was aware of how many expressions of gratitude slipped into her conversation while I was with her. I noticed them. I have noticed them in her letters, too. I've received many of them, faithfully assuring me of her prayers for my work. Some I've kept in a special file; they'll never bring a fortune at an auction, but to me they're priceless. When one of Aletha's letters arrives at the office, other staff members line up to read them. Here's one I got a while ago:

> My Beloved John Haggai,
>
> How thrilling that our Heavenly Father, who knows the end from the beginning, implanted in your youthful heart that intense longing to share your Christ and, finding the fertile soil of dedication, gave you the whole world as your mission field.
>
> Likewise, how glorious that He allowed some of this glow to rub off on to the heart and life of an ordinary little lady longing to find a small place of service to express her devotion for our Lord.
>
> Writing from my bed in Baptist Village infirmary, body broken and stripped of all financial resources, I still love and pray daily for you and your associates—I still have utter space to reach the Throne, and I can still praise Him all the day long.
>
> God bless you,
> Aletha Bergman,
> "Accepted in the Beloved"

Get the Thanksgiving Habit

It's clear why the Smith Effect worked for Aletha Bergman: She got into a habit of thanksgiving.

But the thanksgiving habit is an easy one *not* to get into. Human beings seem to have a natural tendency toward ingratitude. And if history is anything to go by, the greater their prosperity and success, the more ungrateful they get. In Jeremiah 2 the prophet bewails the ingratitude of Israel, who, having received the blessings of the Promised Land, "defiled my land, and made mine heritage an abomination" (Jeremiah 2:7). It was at the moment of King Uzziah's greatness that "his heart was lifted up to his destruction, for he transgressed against the Lord his God" (2 Chronicles 26:16).

People don't change much. We see the same thing happening today, and if we're honest we'll admit to seeing it in our own hearts. We enjoy complaining because it brings us a swift payoff of sympathy. In fact, like Mrs. Smith, we sometimes like sympathy so much that we're willing to buy it with a little real unhappiness.

But how much better not to need sympathy because we have something far more gratifying! James says, "Every good gift and every perfect gift is from above, and cometh down from the Father of lights, with whom is no variableness neither shadow of turning" (James 1:17). We don't have to look to other people for happiness. We don't have to look to ourselves. Our strength is not obtained deep down in the human mind, as humanism would have us believe. Our strength is *Christ*: "In him dwelleth all the fullness of the Godhead bodily" (Colossians 2:9). He gives us all we need—every perfect gift, including the answer to loneliness.

Not only that, but Scripture makes a direct link between thanksgiving and effective prayer: "Be careful for nothing, but in everything by prayer and supplication with thanksgiving let your requests be made known unto God" (Philippians 4:6). "I exhort, therefore, that first of all supplications, prayers, intercessions, and giving of thanks be made for all men" (1 Timothy 2:1).

Many blessings are in store for those who will go back and thank God for what He has already done. Years ago at the Gull Lake Bible Conference, the four-year-old twin granddaughters of the song leader were greeted on the grounds by Mrs. Will Houghton, the late wife of the former president of Moody Bible Institute. She gave them each a pad of paper. A bit later the twins were separated. When they came back together, one noticed that the other had a beautiful pencil.

"Where did you get that pencil?" she asked.

The other answered, "I went back to thank Mrs. Houghton for the pad of paper, and she gave me this pencil."

"Then I think I'll go back and thank Mrs. Houghton for my pad of paper too!"

You may chuckle, but there's an important truth in that little incident. God can give us more blessings if we go back to thank Him for those we've already received.

I hope by now I've said enough to convince you that thanksgiving is beneficial. First, through the "Smith Effect" it transforms our attitude toward experiences both pleasant and unpleasant. Second, as a vital element of prayer it releases extra blessings. But I must be honest and add that besides making you miserable, a refusal to give thanks does a real disservice to the name of Christ. You are saying in effect, "Yes, I'm a Christian, but it's not doing me any good!"

Do you want to be a witness like that? Of course you don't *feel* like giving thanks when you're lonely. But once again, remember that you're dealing in facts, not feelings. The fact is that *Christ is with you.* This means that you have many blessings to be thankful for in spite of your loneliness. So I recommend that you catch the habit of thanksgiving. Thanksgiving to God, in Christ's name, banishes the loneliness blues and infuses into us a divine vitality.

But maybe you don't know where to start. If so, I'll give you some practical hints.

1. *See a new you.* Write a detailed description of your self-image, and look at it carefully. Then write another description—this time not of the way you *are* but of the way you *want*

to be under God: a new you that looks on life with the eye of gratitude, a new you that honors and glorifies the Lord. Keep that "new you" on hand; flash the image on the screen of your mind continuously.

2. *Displace lonely thoughts with thankful thoughts.* You'll never eliminate loneliness (or any other negative trait) simply by saying, "I don't want to be lonely." Negative thoughts need to be replaced, not just removed. Leave an empty space behind them, and they'll soon be back!

Every time you have a lonely thought, counter it with a word of thanks to God. If you like, take five minutes several times a day to review recent events and thank God for them. At the very least, make sure as you retire in the evening that you look back on the day's activities and deliberately thank God for each experience you've been through. It may help if you keep a diary for a few months. If so, make specific entries, even of very simple things like a good meal or a friendly word.

And most important, don't be afraid to confront hard experiences. I guarantee that not one will be without at least the potential for good. If you seem to be on the brink of a disaster, thank God for using this means to drive you to your knees and trust Him more completely.

3. *Express your thanksgiving.* It's good to occupy your mind with thankful thoughts. It's even better to let them spill over into your conversation. Let your verbs become radiant, dynamic verbs and your adjectives become glorious, optimistic adjectives. When someone asks how you feel, don't say "Not bad"; say "Fine, thank you!" And get rid of those grumbles. Imagine what it's like to be on the receiving end of miserable talk like: "I can't find the time to do what's required of me. I'm at the end of my rope, ready to fall apart." Not much fun, is it? So spice it up with some thanksgiving: "God has blessed me with so many opportunities. He's showing me how to set my priorities and how to utilize my time. It's such a glorious experience!"

Back up your words in your actions, your posture, your walk, your facial expressions, and your gestures. Ask yourself: "If I didn't feel lonely, how would I act and speak?" Go back and review that "new you" and think how you can express what God wants and intends you to be. Then begin thanking Him *immediately* that you are developing into that person. Remember—acting thankful will help you *be* thankful. Not only that, but it's a proven fact that people are attracted to others of like attitude. Being thankful will tend to put you in company and situations that encourage thankfulness, giving you positive feedback and making the thanksgiving habit easier.

4. *Let faith grow.* Recognize that adopting the thanksgiving habit makes you use your faith. Faith is like muscle—the more you use it, the stronger it gets. And the stronger your faith is, the more natural it becomes for you to glorify the Lord by giving thanks.

Go to It!

In this chapter I have tried to demonstrate how getting right with God through the thanksgiving habit neutralizes loneliness. It's only the first step in your program, but I think you'll find that it yields some positive results. So are you ready to put it into practice? If so, take a pencil right now and go back through the chapter, writing down a simple plan that fits your own particular circumstances. Then put it into action for three weeks. Stick faithfully to your discipline, and after 21 days you'll notice two changes. First, your loneliness will seem a smaller problem. And second, your relationships with other people will take a distinct turn for the better.

But don't wait three weeks before going on to Chapter 8!

8

Be Alone With God

Psalm 91 begins, "He that dwelleth in the secret place of the Most High shall abide under the shadow of the Almighty" (Psalm 91:1).

It's a psalm which the lonely person would do well to read. No one who abides under the shadow of the Almighty will linger for long in the shadows of loneliness. In God's presence there is deliverance "from the snare of the fowler and from the noisome pestilence." God, pictured like a strong eagle, spreads out His feathers to cover those who trust Him, so they need fear neither "the terror by night nor . . . the arrow that flieth by day."

To abide in the shadow of God is to make Him our habitation, our fortress and shelter. The solitude feared by many lonely people need not be absolute solitude, but solitude spent in the presence of God. In that place the divine promises pour out in torrents, transforming lonely wastelands into fertile farms, and unbearable quietness into wholesome stillness of heart, mind, and soul. Do you fear solitude? If you do, make up your mind to change your attitude right now. Solitude is not a pain, but a resource—an opportunity to gain the strength that only God can give you. As the Scripture says, "They that wait upon the Lord shall renew their strength; they shall mount up with wings as eagles; they shall run and not be weary; and they shall walk and not faint" (Isaiah 40:31).

God's voice is rarely heard in the cacophony of human interaction, or the prattle of the media, or the deafening roar of corporate psychoanalysis. His is the quiet voice that spoke to Elijah in the cave at Horeb. To hear it requires solitude. How many times do we read in the Gospels that Jesus went apart? And did He not request the same of His followers?

91

Even in the Old Testament the man of God arose in the hours before dawn. Why? To be alone with God.

I am convinced that victory demands a certain amount of solitude. King David said, "The Lord will hear when I call unto him. Stand in awe, and sin not; commune with your own heart upon your bed, and be still" (Psalm 4:3,4).

Years ago, just before his death, 92-year-old J. C. Massee pointed out that passage to me, and said: "If you're going to be a man of God and a leader of men, it is mandatory that you spend a great deal of time alone." I pass on this sage counsel to the lonely person. Victory will not come without seclusion, time spent communing with yourself in the presence of God, talking to Him and letting Him speak to you. Even a secular leader has emphasized the value of being alone: "Decisions that are made after long periods of meditation, without undue reference to the whims of others, have the uncanny quality of being almost 100 percent right."

The "whims of others" exercise an extraordinary power over the lonely person. Someone gripped by loneliness will feel isolated from those who seem to live happier lives than he does, and as a result he will usually give credence to anyone who offers to cure him. And there's no shortage of cures! The Platonist says, "Man, know thyself." The Stoic says, "Man, rule thyself." The humanist says, "Man, improve thyself." The Buddhist says, "Man, annihilate thyself." The Moslem says, "Man, submit thyself." The twentieth-century internationalist says, "Man, learn the art of peaceful coexistence."

In contrast, Christ says, "Without me ye can do nothing" (John 15:5). It is *in communion with Christ* that we gain the strength to win over not just loneliness but every other challenge that faces us. Without Him we are helpless, but with Him nothing is impossible!

I tell you frankly that from the Psalms, from the journal of John Wesley, from the biography of John Mott, from the observation of my father's lifestyle, and from my own personal experience, I have concluded that nothing is more important to emotional vitality, psychological resilience, mental creativity, and spiritual strength than those hours spent alone with God. So don't be afraid of solitude. Cherish it, and learn the joy of using your previously lonely hours to fellowship with the Lord. In particular, set about organizing your quiet time.

What Is a Quiet Time?

A quiet time, or "devotions," is essential for getting right with God because it allows God access to your life.

What kind of marriage would a woman have if she never had time alone with her husband? Not a very satisfying one at all. Human beings need time together, talking and listening, if their relationships are going to grow and deepen. It's the same with God. To fill out your friendship with God, you cannot do without talking to Him and listening as He talks to you. These two activities—talking and listening—are the fundamental elements of a "quiet time." For simplicity I'll call them "prayer" and "meditation."

Many people claim they don't have room in the day for a quiet time. If you are the Top Dog, you're probably thinking that right now! But let me ask you this: Can you honestly say that anything you do is more important than spending time with God? If you can, you'd better take a long, hard look at your priorities. If you can't, get your diary out and start looking for a suitable slot. Don't make the excuse that your day is already booked. If the President of the United States asked to see you tomorrow, wouldn't you see him? If so, what are you doing deferring God's appointment to a more convenient time? Appointments with God are never wasted. In fact I find my devotions to be timesaving. Waiting upon God in the morning assures me of a day lived wisely for the glory of the Lord.

I myself find the early morning most suitable. Of course there are no hard-and-fast rules. A mother may want to wait until later in the day, when the kids are at school and she has time to relax. Some people have their quiet time late in the evening. If that really suits you—fine. What matters is not the exact time and place, but that you can really give yourself to prayer and meditation on God. Nonetheless, because a quiet time must be done regularly and systematically and will always require discipline and concentration, I strongly recommend the beginning of the day. There aren't likely to be many distractions if the rest of the household is still asleep!

In addition to your quiet time, it's a good idea to add short moments of meditation during the rest of the day. Meet God in your coffee break at the office, over lunch, or when you're driving. If you can't manage to isolate yourself physically, try to cultivate a sense of aloneness with God at your office desk, in the kitchen or the supermarket, in a coffee shop or airport. Remember, in order to pray effectively you don't need to adopt any special body position. Kneeling doesn't bring more blessing than sitting—in fact you may find sitting more comfortable and less distracting. You can pray quite satisfactorily walking along the street!

"But what do I *do* when I pray?" you ask.

Well, I'm not about to give you a list of how-to's. When the disciples came to Jesus they didn't say, "Lord, teach us *how* to pray." They just said, "Lord, teach us to pray." Prayer isn't something you learn as a technique. It is an encounter with God that takes place solely on the basis of faith. (For anyone seeking more help on the practicalities of prayer, I recommend Chapters 21-24 of my book *How to Win Over Worry.*)

Jesus replied to the disciples' question by saying, "When ye pray, say . . ." and then gave them what we know as the Lord's Prayer. That prayer gives us no hint of technique. It wasn't necessarily meant as a prayer to be memorized and repeated, though Christians often use it like that. Rather, the Lord's Prayer sketches out an attitude in which the believer is to approach the throne of grace, and acts as a heavenly guideline for all prayer.

The object of prayer is that we should get to know God, and develop a longing to know Him still better. Faithful prayer is self-perpetuating—it produces a desire in us to deepen our relationship with the Lord, expand our understanding of His

Word, and spend more time with Him in solitude. This deep desire for intimate fellowship with God was beautifully expressed by an elderly lady who stayed in church long after the service was over. When asked why she stayed behind when everyone else had gone home, she smiled and said, "I just want to look into the beautiful face of my God."

She was an inheritor of one of the rich promises of Jesus: "Blessed are they which do hunger and thirst after righteousness, for they shall be filled" (Matthew 5:6).

Meditation True and False

It's hard to use the word "meditation" today without thinking of Eastern religions.

The most famous of them, Transcendental Meditation, has swept the Western world. Many claims are made for it. According to Montague Guild, Jr., president of Guild Investment Management, from a purely financial point of view TM is the hottest innovation in business management since the industrial revolution. His own experience of it came during a decade in which his investment success was meteoric.

There is now an organization committed to "evangelizing" America's business community with the benefits of TM. They claim that TM produces greater efficiency, a dramatic rise in creative expression, and measurable job improvement, not to mention physical and psychological advantages. Some companies seem to have taken the claims seriously: Monsanto Chemicals, Sunnydale Milk Farms, Xerox, and Connecticut General Life Insurance have all allegedly sponsored TM programs.

The basis of TM is the use of the mantra—a group of sounds assigned secretly and individually to each practitioner. The mantra allegedly has no meaning, but its silent repetition while the body is in a state of rest is said to facilitate nervous functions, improve the metabolism, and neutralize stress. Prolonged use, it is suggested, can make more efficient use of the practitioner's mental capacity.

Such claims may or may not be true, but TM's concept of meditation differs widely from that of the Bible. In fact, I would assert that TM is not only unnecessary for Christians but is a diabolical counterfeit of the true meditation available to the child of God through the devotional life as outlined in Scripture. The promotion of TM as a "nonreligious" practice is deception pure and simple: TM shares much of the theology of Hinduism, and Hindu deities are specifically honored in the initiation ceremony in which the practitioner is given his mantra.

On top of that, the technique of meditation used in TM seeks to achieve a neutral or blank state of mind. This is in stark contrast to Christian meditation, where the focus is not blankness but the very Person of God. A brilliant scholar, Chinese Singaporian, and former Haggai Institute Assistant Dean Ah Tua Teo says: "One may liken TM to a stick floating on a calm, stagnant pond. However, in Christ-centered meditation the life becomes like a stick that stands against a rushing, mighty torrent. In other words, it has a vital and positive contribution even when one is back in the stress of life's pressures."

True meditation does not seek to achieve a certain mental state by the use of a certain technique. It brings you into contact with the Creator God in just the same way as prayer, with the exception that by meditating you put yourself into a "receiving" mode. You probably won't hear God audibly, though some claim to have heard Him in that way. More often He speaks by giving sharp insights and impressions, stirring up memories of past blessing, and illuminating His Word. God's written Word, the Bible, has always had this role. Joshua was instructed to soak himself in it that he might be directed in the right way:

> This book of the law shall not depart out of thy mouth; but thou shalt meditate therein day and night, that thou mayest observe to do according to all that is written therein, for then thou shalt make thy way prosperous and then thou shalt have good success (Joshua 1:8).

Time and again in the Psalms we find the writer meditating on the Lord's Word:

His delight is in the law of the Lord, and in His law doth he meditate day and night (Psalm 1:2).

Thy word is a lamp unto my feet and a light unto my path (Psalm 119:105).

Sometimes meditation allows God to speak to us on very specific issues. I remember taking several days off my usual work to meditate in the Lord's presence. I had the inkling of an idea that God had a plan for advanced leadership training in the Third World. The vision that God gave me during those few days gave birth to the Haggai Institute, and still continues to inspire an ever-expanding program of training in evangelism.

At other times meditation brings into our minds not God's plans for us but simply God Himself. At this point meditation can move us to respond with thanksgiving and praise for what He has done for us. The German theologian Bengel, who had a reputation as a great man of prayer, was seen one day reading a large Bible. He stopped often, meditating with silent tears running down his cheeks. After a long period of reading, Bengel closed the Book and began to speak to God. His meditation had thoroughly prepared him for prayer.

Getting Started

Perhaps you would like to have a quiet time with the Lord, but don't know how to go about it. If so, I offer a few practical suggestions to help you maximize the potential of your quiet time.

First, set a definite time each day which you determine to keep with inviolable punctuality. Even if you sometimes get to bed late and are inclined to sleep in the next morning, I would suggest that you still get up for your quiet time and then, if necessary, go back to bed or take a nap later in the afternoon. Failure to maintain a definite time and place each day weakens the resolve and increases the probability of inconsistency.

Second, have some system of Bible reading to get you familiar with the Scriptures. There are many ways of doing it. You can read through the whole Bible from beginning to end. You can read through the Old Testament and the New Testament concurrently. Or you might like to read a chapter, then add a psalm to help you in your devotions, and a chapter from Proverbs to help you in your relationships.

Personally, though I like to keep up-to-date in my coverage of both Testaments, I tend to read the New more often than the Old. But I don't always read the New Testament in the same way. My "problem" is the large quantity of duplication between the Gospels, and I solve it by using only one at a time: I go through Matthew, Mark, Luke, and John not all together but individually in four successive readings.

Third, don't worry if your mind wanders. It happens to everyone, and if you start feeling guilty about it you'll only end up being distracted all the more. God understands your weaknesses. Provided you don't start out with the intention of daydreaming, there's no great harm done!

Fourth, don't be put off by passages in the Bible that you can't make sense of. Don't let them annoy you or discourage you—just look to the Lord for enlightenment and trust that He will teach you in good time. Abraham Lincoln said, "I accept what I can by reason, and the rest I accept by faith until the day that reason catches up with faith."

Fifth, keep a notebook handy. If anything strikes you during your Bible reading, write it down. You may want to refer to it later.

Sixth, when you've finished reading, quietly relax for a moment before the Lord, meditating on the fact that He is with you—ready, willing, and able to meet your every need. He will even meet your desires if you qualify. The qualification? Delight in the Lord: "Delight thyself also in the Lord, and he shall give thee the desires of thine heart."

Seventh, go to prayer. Open your heart to the Lord, and spread out your petitions before Him.

I find two items useful in prayer. One is a prayer list. This is especially handy when my mind wanders and I need to get back on track. I have three columns on my prayer list. The prayer item goes in the middle. In the left column I enter the date I began to pray for it, and in the right column the date the prayer was answered. I have received many wonderful and specific answers, and when I look at that right column packed with dates my faith is strengthened and I am filled with gratitude to God. The prayer list not only reminds me what to pray for but acts as a stimulus to thanksgiving. Of course, not every prayer is answered immediately. For example, I am praying for patience. God has done a wonderful work in my life in that regard, but I am still far from being a truly patient person!

The second item I find useful is the notepad. I use it as a kind of "Out Box." Often during my prayer time a matter will come to mind that requires attention later in the day. Writing it down both acts as a memo and stops me from thinking about it when I should be praying.

One final word: Just because you've stopped reading and started praying doesn't mean you stop listening.

My father has always been up before daybreak for his quiet time. As a boy I wondered what on earth he could find to say—after all, he was sometimes on his knees for two whole hours. But when I asked him he simply said, "I don't do all the talking."

Be alert to God's voice and sensitive to His impressions.

Eighth and last, don't practice centrifugal prayer—in other words, don't always be thinking about yourself and the people you know. If you love God you must pray for all His children, regardless of their language, location, color, or culture. Remember, Scripture includes a specific command to pray for *all* men:

> I exhort therefore that first of all supplications,
> prayers, intercessions, and giving of thanks be

made for all men: for kings and for all that are in
authority, that we may lead a quiet and peaceable
life in all godliness and honesty (1 Timothy 2:1,2).

Getting right with God means getting the habit of thanksgiving, and using your solitude to be in the company of God.
You'll find the two very complementary. Both have direct
practical value in combating loneliness, and both are helped
by a third element in getting right with God—*contentment*.
Read on!

9

The Contented Christian

In Chapter 3 I identified discontent as one of three conditions characterizing loneliness as a sin.

Discontent is a trap that the lonely person easily falls into because, being lonely, he feels he has something to be discontented about. Take the example of a woman alone in a big house, her children grown up and living elsewhere, her husband tied up with a demanding career. She is now deprived of her role as mother. Her husband often works late. She is left facing long, empty days, yet she feels inadequate to take up a new social life. Discontent arises out of her loneliness, and also out of the circumstances that have produced that loneliness. She starts as the Lonely-in-Love and soon winds up as the Ugly Duckling.

Believe me, I have no wish to belittle the power of circumstance. There's hardly anyone in this world for whom the grass hasn't occasionally seemed greener on the far side of the valley. I think of those who serve much and are compensated little, of the women who want to go to college but are immobilized by the illness of a loved one. I think of men with empires in their brains who, because of high blood pressure, must restrict their activities to one hour a day. As the father of a wonderful son who for the 24 years of his life suffered the ravages of cerebral palsy, I think particularly of those given the hard calling of raising a handicapped child.

Such situations, among many others, surely justify discontent. Or do they? Listen to what Paul the apostle said of his situation in the last stage of his life:

> I am now ready to be offered, and the time of my
> departure is at hand. . . . Demas hath forsaken me,
> having loved this present world, and is departed

> unto Thessalonica, Crescens to Galatia, Titus unto Dalmatia. Only Luke is with me. . . . At my first answer no man stood with me, but all men forsook me; I pray God that it may not be laid to their charge (2 Timothy 4:6,10,11,16).

Here was a man with much to complain of. After years of suffering for the sake of the gospel he had been arrested, imprisoned, and taken to Rome for trial. Nearly all his friends had deserted him. At his trial he had stood alone. But was Paul discontented? Read an excerpt from his letter to the Philippians, written around the same period:

> I have learned in whatsoever state I am, therewith to be content. I know both how to be abased and I know how to abound; everywhere and in all things I am instructed both to be full and to be hungry, both to abound and to suffer need. I can do all things through Christ which strengtheneth me (Philippians 4:11-13).

The answer is clearly no. In spite of every discomfort and every deprivation, Paul felt thoroughly content. He didn't regret the loss of his freedom, or pine for the wealth and respect that could have been his had he remained a Pharisee: "What things were gain to me, those I counted loss for Christ" (Philippians 3:7). Christ alone was enough. Nothing else compared. "That I may know him and the power of his resurrection" was the goal for which Paul was willing to pay any price.

Such contentment is largely a forgotten virtue today. Instead we are obsessed by the desire for improvement. Keeping up with the Joneses is often of more interest to us than developing a robust Christian spirituality. Yet our grandparents were content to honeymoon in the next farmhouse or relax with a walk in the country, and they had just as good a time as we do. So the idea that we never have enough to make us happy is a fallacy. The more we have, it seems, the less happy we are!

Learn to be content, whatever your lot. Don't let the world brainwash you into dissatisfaction. Don't let the fashion magazines persuade you that your effectiveness in society varies in proportion to the style of your clothes. Turn a deaf ear to the advertisers who tell you that home entertaining is impossible without the latest patio furniture or designer kitchenware. Defy the television media's constant insinuation that good looks are essential for happiness and success. Be content with what God has given you.

Contentment isn't the same as apathy; being content won't stop you from achieving. But it will stop you from being the kind of person nobody likes—a complainer. Complainers have nothing to talk about but problems. Their world is so full of problems that there's no room for anything else. They are unhappy, and their unhappiness saps their strength and drives other people away from them. In contrast, contentment fosters optimism and effectiveness. It makes us strong in Christ and independent of our outward circumstances.

Remember, however tough life seems, God will never abandon you. I know that from the experience of my own family.

In 1931 I was a seven-year-old boy living with my parents in Kalamazoo, Michigan. During the worst blizzard in Michigan's history there occurred an event that has been etched indelibly into my memory. Dad's preaching had earned him nothing for several weeks. One day we came down for breakfast. The table was set but there was no food on it. The fire was burning but there was no more fuel—no wood, no coal, no coke.

We sat down. I remember that Dad read the Scripture as usual, and then we had prayer. He prayed for the missionaries of the cross, our relatives both saved and unsaved, our neighbors, the members of our church, and the affairs of our family. Then he went on something like this:

"Lord, Thou knowest there is no food except eight ounces of milk for Baby Tom. Thou knowest there is no more fuel for the fire. If it is Thy will that we not eat today, we will with gratitude accept that as Thy best for our lives. If it is Thy will that we have no heat, we thank Thee for the warm clothes Thou hast provided and for the warm bed, and we will accept from Thy hand that which Thou dost give, or we will accept as Thy best for us that which Thou dost withhold."

Well, possibly because I was the oldest child, I was always the most sensitive to the family's financial position, and I must say I wasn't as contented as Dad appeared to be. But hardly had we come to the end of the prayer when there was a noise at the front of the house. We could tell by the sound that someone had driven up with horses and a sleigh. There was a pounding at the door. With much effort my father pulled the door free from its icy seal, and the snow came tumbling in.

There was a man outside.

"Reverend," he said, "you may not remember me, but I heard you preach in Allegan, Michigan, some time ago. This morning the Lord awakened me with you on my mind. I couldn't drive my truck because of the roads, so I hooked up the horses to the sleigh, and I just felt impelled to bring this to you."

Then he gave Dad two large bags of groceries, a cord of wood, and ten dollars.

I shall never forget that experience. In difficult circumstances today, the memory of it reinforces my own contentment and banishes any temptation to loneliness.

Part 3

GET RIGHT WITH YOURSELF

10

Thought Control

Years ago when I was at college, my wife and I stayed with a high school math teacher.

He was a dear man of great compassion. He was never harsh in criticism. When asked for an appraisal of another person he would respond with only two comments. He would either say "He has a good attitude" or "He has a bad attitude."

At the time I considered this a superficial method of assessing people. Thirty-five years later I am convinced he was right. A person's *attitude* is one of the fundamental determinants of success, not just in math but in any task that a human being takes on. The rudiments of success are to be found in the mind. It is a principle written in the pages of Scripture. "As a man thinketh in his heart," the writer of Proverbs tells us, "so is he" (Proverbs 23:7). The old adage makes the same point: "You are what you think."

No one can live a joyous life if his mind is full of lonely thoughts. What is inside you will always express itself. Think thoughts of loneliness and you will upset your mental well-being and ultimately your physical well-being. Because your mind is linked to every part of you, it's only natural that when you feel below-par mentally you'll start to feel below-par physically. That's the definition of *psychosomatic* illness—a manifestation in the body (Greek *soma*) of what is happening in the mind (Greek *psyche*).

The wife of one of America's assassinated presidents was a bedridden paralytic for years. Her husband waited on her hand and foot, even when he worked in the White House. She seemed to take great delight in ringing a bell to summon him when he was in the middle of an important meeting. Yet after his death she got up and lived a perfectly normal life.

What was the cause of her invalidism? Her mind, of course. As some of those who knew the couple said later, she was in competition with her husband: She was jealous of all the attention he received, and she made her presence felt—probably quite unconsciously—through sickness.

Reprogram Your Mind

Think of your mind as the internal computer that runs your whole person. It is a wonderful, intricate piece of apparatus. But just like a real computer, it has to be given the right program if it's going to do its job. Getting right with yourself, therefore, begins with putting the correct program into your "computer."

You may think your mind is so much a law unto itself that imposing any sort of control over it is impossible. I assure you it is not. If most people have disorganized, random minds, that's because they haven't taken the trouble to use them properly. The fact is that it's no harder to control what goes into your mind than what goes into your body. When lunchtime comes around you don't open the refrigerator and stuff the contents indiscriminately into your mouth (at least I hope you don't!). Eating is an organized activity. You eat at certain times, and you try to get a balanced diet. And you do that because you know that what you eat affects your overall health.

The same motive should apply to your mind. Good thinking means good living and good emotional and physical health. Ella Wilcox Wheeler puts it aptly in her poem *Secret Thoughts*:

> I hold it true that thoughts are things
> Endowed with bodies, breath and wings,
> And that we send them forth to fill
> The world with good results or ill.
>
> That which we call our secret thought
> Speeds to the earth's remotest spot,

And leaves its blessings or its woes
Like tracks behind it as it goes.

It is God's law. Remember it
In your still chamber as you sit
With thoughts you would not dare have known
And yet make comrades when alone.

These thoughts have life; and they will fly
And leave their impress by and by,
Like some marsh breeze, whose poisoned breath
Breathes into homes its fevered breath.

And after you have quite forgot
Or all outgrown some vanished thought,
Back to your mind to make its home,
A dove or raven, it will come.

Then let your secret thoughts be fair;
They have a vital part and share
In shaping worlds and molding fate—
God's system is so intricate.

Be careful what you allow to go into the new program for your mind! It's easy to accept ideas that seem encouraging and helpful but are really destructive intruders. I tell the secretaries at our offices to be sure to lock their car doors day and night—not because I want to instill fear, but as a wise precaution. You probably do the same with your car. But if you are vigilant in protecting your *property*, how much more vigilant should you be in protecting your *mind*? Make no mistake—there are negative, loneliness-inducing thoughts standing at the door of your consciousness, waiting to gain admittance.

God won't protect you from thoughts like that. You can quote all you like from passages such as Psalm 91—"He shall give his angels charge over thee, to keep thee in all thy ways . . . lest thou dash thy foot against a stone" (Psalm 91:11,12). The psalmist isn't advocating that you run across a field of rocks in bare feet. The condition of God's help is that you exercise a bit of common sense in avoiding avoidable problems! You don't take medication without checking the label on the bottle. You don't just assume that your children will choose the right friends or make the right decisions without guidance and sound training. Doing stupid things in the belief that God will protect you isn't faith—it's presumption.

So take care not to be dragged into consensus thinking. Analyze the ideas you're receiving from the media. Be cautious in your choice of books, magazines, and TV programs. Watch out for the times when you dwell on gloomy, depressing, or lonely themes. Everything you let your mind concentrate on will influence you, whether you like it or not. If you don't want to pick up bad influences, make sure you avoid them, just like you would avoid visiting a place with a smallpox epidemic. Your aim should be to have every thought under your control, every thought doing what you want it to do. As Paul said, "Casting down imaginations, and every high thing that exalteth itself against the knowledge of God, and bringing into captivity every thought to the obedience of Christ" (2 Corinthians 10:5).

In particular, be careful what kind of company you keep. Generally, the person you spend the most time with will have the greatest influence over your thinking. A negative person will program your mind negatively. Be on your guard against that. If you spend time with people who disparage the things of God or project cynical opinions, think carefully about your priorities. Real friendship is never bought with the betrayal of your principles; attempting to win the approval of scoffing acquaintances by accommodating their ideas will often cast a lonely Christian into greater depths of loneliness. In cases like that, standing alone—deliberately being the Outsider—is the true road to success. Anything less is really a sellout. You would be saying, "The unspeakable gift, the Lord Jesus Christ, my Savior, is not adequate to give me the strength to cope with these pressures." Of course He is adequate! In fact there's no winning over loneliness without Him, no getting right with yourself or with others without first getting right with God.

Of course reprogramming your mind isn't just a matter of avoiding negative influences. If indifferent company is a danger, it stands to reason that good company is a help. The apostle Paul said to Titus that a church leader should be a "lover of good men" (Titus 1:8), which is sound advice to anyone. Fellowship with positive, Spirit-filled, Christ-centered people will assist you in programming your mind because it will surround you with positive affirmations. How do you recognize a good person? Read a few of the key features as laid down by Scripture. A good person is:

1. Content whatever his situation (Philippians 4:11).
2. Always rejoicing in the Lord (Philippians 4:4).
3. Ready to give thanks in all things (1 Thessalonians 5:18).
4. Confident that he has all and abounds (Philippians 4:18).
5. Living abundantly (John 10:10).

Seek out people like that. Positive Christian fellowship is one of the riches you enjoy as a child of the King, one of your privileges as a member of God's family. Use that privilege. Paul was not ashamed to tell the churches he had founded to imitate him in the faith. So if you find Christians who, like Paul, lead lives worthy of imitation, use them as models to reprogram your mind.

Try to resist negative thoughts and ideas by leaving no room for them. Fill your mind with the good, the wholesome, the honest, the uplifting. Reject negative thoughts but welcome the positive. That was Paul's parting advice to the Philippians:

Finally, brethren, whatsoever things are true, whatsoever things are honest, whatsoever things are just, whatsoever things are pure, whatsoever things are lovely, whatsoever things are of good report; if there be any virtue, and if there be any praise, think on these things (Philippians 4:8).

At first thought control will take a little effort. But with practice it can soon become a way of life.

Anybody who knows Charlie "Tremendous" Jones will tell you he is an unusual fellow. Charlie is the author of *Life Is Tremendous* and an acclaimed speaker on leadership. More striking, though, is the fact that he never complains, never gripes or frets. Can't believe it? Nor could I. Yet this high-powered blend of optimism, positivism, and faith seemed to be running in overdrive all the time.

One evening after Charlie and I had done a long day together at the same meeting, he asked me to ride with him from Philadelphia to Harrisburg. It was a little past midnight. Normally I would have preferred the plane, but I accepted because I thought I might learn more about him. Years ago I found that if you want to really know about a man, you should stay up with him late at night. In the fight against sleep he will let his guard slip; he will speak more freely and let out pieces of information that he would usually conceal. I was curious to have that experience with Charlie "Tremendous" Jones.

I don't know what Charlie found out about me, but after that midnight-to-dawn journey I can tell you that no matter how dog-tired that man might be, he is as upbeat, as positive, as ready to rejoice as the minute he wakes up in the morning. He has reprogrammed his mind effectively. For years he has honored Christ by depositing in his memory vaults the kinds of thoughts and ideas that bring praise to God, and those thoughts bring him profit and blessing.

Another person like that is Carl Newton, head of Fox-Stanley Photo Products, Inc., in San Antonio, Texas, one of America's most respected businessmen. I always enjoy hearing him pray in family devotions. He spends as high a percentage of prayer time in thanking the Lord specifically for various blessings and gifts as any person I have ever known.

When you've been with Carl at family prayers, you leave refreshed. If you were a little on the ragged edge when you came in, you leave with a spring in your step!

Yet Carl and his lovely wife, Janie, lost their teenage daughter a few years ago. She came home from school feeling sick one afternoon and was dead the next day. It came as a terrible shock, and in one way they've never really gotten over it. But to be with them you would never know they had endured such sorrow. They program themselves positively. They will to keep moving, keep growing, keep blessing.

The Place to Start

Let's talk about some of the procedures I've found useful in reprogramming the mind for God's glory.

First, determine what kind of thoughts you want dominating your mind, and start storing them in your memory.

For inspiration I suggest that you look at Scripture, since there is no better source of positive thoughts. Take Philippians 4:13—"I can do all things through Christ which strengtheneth me." Dr. Jesse Henley's translation of that is: "I am almighty in the One who continually keeps pouring His power in me." What do I do to get this in my mind? Simple. I write it down on a card and repeat it over and over. When I'm going through a difficult time and I'm tempted to brood, or to blame my circumstances and other people, I quote the passage to myself—not once, but several times. Fifty or a hundred times isn't too many!

You'll always find a few moments in your day when you can repeat a passage of Scripture. You can do it after the kids have gone to school or when you're driving to work. Put your card on the sun visor in the car so you can see it when you stop at a light. Leave it by your bed to remind you of it last thing at night. If it won't upset the family, use soap to write it on one of the bathroom mirrors, or record it on cassette and play it while you're doing the housecleaning!

Second, examine your own situation and find positive affirmations to suit it.

You can do this easily by adapting the affirmations of Scripture to your own situation. Philippians 4:19 says, "My God shall supply all your need according to his riches in glory by Christ Jesus." You can shorten that to "Through Christ, God is providing for all my needs." On the other hand, you can expand it to be more specific: "Through Christ, God is providing for all my needs—mental needs, physical needs, financial needs, spiritual needs, family needs. God is providing for them all."

If you are inclined to brood over loneliness, make yourself a card reading: "My social requirements are fully met in the companionship of Christ and those whom He has brought into my life." That is biblical truth even if it isn't expressed in biblical words, and it is the kind of deposit you want to lay up in the vault of your memory. Remember, God will use what is stored in your memory to program your subconscious mind. Right now your idle moments may give rise to random or ribald thoughts, because that's all you've got stored inside. But take a little time learning verses, and you'll find that they return to enrich you when you least expect it.

There is no situation that cannot be improved by reprogramming the mind in this way. Older people, for example, suffer loneliness on two fronts—first because most of their friends have died, and second because they can easily feel neglected and useless. Yet an elderly person will benefit enormously from using the right positive affirmations: "I am making new friends; this is a stimulating experience both for me and for my new friends" or "I am using my years of experience to encourage younger people. I don't dote on the past, but I look to God for wisdom as I creatively pass on helpful suggestions without meddling or pressuring."

Use positive affirmations to assault your weaknesses and maximize your opportunities.

Third, be what you affirm.

A stockbroker in the City of London will often have a plaque hanging in the office saying "Be aware." The sign encourages him too maintain the state of mind necessary to increase the efficiency of his work. I've noticed similar signs in the offices of many outstanding leaders—mottoes or epigrams on framed papers, parchments, or hammered metals, all designed to let the person program his mind with the thoughts he feels are essential and productive.

It's a way of talking to yourself, and it requires no particular gifts and no great wealth—not even time. When you come to think about it, we program ourselves (or allow ourselves to be programmed) every moment of our lives. So it requires little effort to ensure that the programming is positive instead of negative.

When I was in Portugal on a crusade in 1972 I learned the Portuguese for "I am happy in the Lord"—"*Sto contente no Senor.*" It proved extremely useful, as the crowds arriving at the Sports Pavilion each night looked harried and burdened. I asked them to repeat the phrase with me—"Sto contente no Senor." At first they did it rather perfunctorily, so the second time around I asked them to put more expression into the words, to say it with their faces as well as their lips. By the third attempt this simple exercise in self-programming had transformed the atmosphere.

The fact is that merely voicing a positive affirmation changes the way we feel, and with a little concentration we can turn that characteristic to our advantage. At the outset, affirming facts by faith—in the teeth of the evidence—may seem hard, even a mockery. But provided those affirmations are rooted in the eternal truth of the Word of God, we will certainly realize them in our experience. Psychology has demonstrated time and again that a human being will tend to accommodate to his self-image. A negative, lonely self-image reinforces loneliness. Tell yourself you're lonely, and you will *be* lonely. But picture yourself as "abounding in all things" and you will start to find peace, joy, and fulfillment.

You are what you think. So link up your thinking with the facts of your situation as laid bare in the promises of God. Those promises are a natural incentive to thanksgiving, and that thanksgiving will help you get right with God. But the promises are also the ground on which you restore your relationship with yourself. No business will expand while the directors think it's on the verge of bankruptcy. Expansion requires a healthy recognition of economic strength. In the same way, you will not win over loneliness until you program your mind to see what blessings you have already received. You are not alone; God is with you. He has put you in the company of His saints. So get those thoughts under control and start winning over loneliness!

11

Adjust That Rearview Mirror!

Thought control is the most effective way to get a handle on your present circumstances. But of course not all circumstances are "present." In fact very few of them are: Like intersections on a highway, circumstances are seen a long way off and remembered when they're long gone, but are actually experienced only in the split second we pass them. As travelers on the road of life we are perpetually stuck between the journey behind and the journey ahead—between past and future.

On a real highway we can rectify past mistakes by backtracking. But we can't do that with life; it's a truism that the past cannot be changed. We cannot unsay a thoughtless remark any more than we can bring back the dead. Our words and actions are written indelibly in the pages of history, and they play their part in deciding what will be written here and now.

For some people that is a depressing thought. But it need not be. Certainly the past influences us, but it is only one influence among many. And past misdemeanors can be countered even when they cannot be undone. We demonstrate that fact every time we apologize for hurting another person's feelings or think twice about an ill-advised decision. The real danger, especially with a problem like loneliness, is that the past becomes poisoned with the emotions of the present. Everyone's past experience is a mixed bag. There is good and bad, happiness and sorrow, the light of grace and the shadow of sin. But the fact that you've blotted your study notes is no excuse for throwing them in the garbage. If you reject your past as a lost cause, you are doing it a disservice. More than that, you are insulting God.

God means our past to be a resource, a reservoir of memories to encourage and inspire us. You may say, "That's all very well for you to say, but you don't have a past like mine!" Well, I probably do. I've made my fair share of mistakes and had my fair share of problems and pain. But that doesn't stop me from seeing the hand of God in it. If you are a lonely person it is quite true that you have all kinds of lonely memories, but they are not the problem. The problem is that you refuse to see anything else!

After God had granted Israel a decisive victory over the Philistines, the prophet Samuel set up a memorial stone called Ebenezer, saying "Hitherto hath the Lord helped us." He could have called it something else and said, "Hitherto have we had a real tough fight!" That wouldn't have been untrue. But neither would it have done full justice to Israel's past at that point. The most important fact was not how hard the struggle had been but that the Lord had been with them. Recalling the struggle would bring them no consolation; remembering God's help would bring them plenty of encouragement.

Samuel was using memory in exactly the right way. He commemorated the victory of Israel in God's strength. Never again did the Philistines prevail over Israel during Samuel's lifetime. I believe that the memory instituted by Samuel undergirded Israel's faith, and that God acted accordingly. Their right view of the past actually facilitated blessing in the present. God was honored when they reflected on His deeds; they rejoiced in Him, and in that rejoicing God delivered them.

The principle stands: If we are prepared to see the hand of God in our yesterdays, then we are ready to receive His blessing in our todays. Taking a positive view of the past helps free us from feelings of depression and bitterness. We see it through a wide-angle lens—God's strength and our failure all in the same frame. We have no excuse for thinking we were abandoned in our moment of need or made to fight alone against impossible odds. On the contrary, by looking back we see that God was right at our side even in the worst situations. And that knowledge boosts our faith for the present. Has He been with you in six troubles? He will be with you in the seventh.

In *How to Win Over Pain* I mentioned a remarkable man whom my father met years ago in Pittsburgh, Pennsylvania—Dr. Blair. He was a Presbyterian minister who was blind and dependent for mobility on his Seeing Eye dog. He had more cause for loneliness than most of us, yet he was a radiant man, so much so that people at my father's church competed for the chance to chat with him.

He lost one of his eyes during his tenure as a missionary in India. It literally popped out. The doctor told him that because of pressure building up behind the other eye he would soon lose that as well, and this happened shortly after his return to the States with his family. Blindness is hard enough for anyone to bear, but Dr. Blair's problems had just begun. A few months after he lost his second eye his wife died, leaving behind the handicapped daughter whose care had now become his responsibility. Not long after that one of his sons came in contact with poison from bushes during a cross-country race. He too died. Finally, the Seeing Eye dog was fatally injured by a hit-and-run driver. Dr. Blair's other son, who had been taking the dog for a walk, was lucky to escape unhurt.

That night Dr. Blair listened to the injured animal groaning in pain under the bed, and cried out to the Lord, "O God, can't I even have my dog?" But the dog died, and Dr. Blair arranged the funeral. The text he used was: "The Lord giveth, and the Lord taketh away. Blessed be the name of the Lord." It was extremely moving. This man had lost some of the most precious gifts he had—his sight, his wife, one of his sons, and the dog who took him around. Totally blind, he was saddled with the care of a handicapped child whom a seeing person would have been hard-pressed to look after. Yet he remained radiant. Why?

One of the reasons is that Dr. Blair used his memories wisely. He regularly reviewed God's blessings. He knew that the Lord who had been with him in six troubles would be with him in the seventh. And he shared the blessings of his past experiences with friends and audiences everywhere.

It is a strange fact that a landscape can look more breathtaking in the rearview mirror than it did through the windshield. Perhaps that is because when you look back you see the same scene from a different angle. Memories are like that. If you keep your rearview mirror clean and use it wisely, you may feel your spirit soaring over experiences that at the time seemed modest and unexciting.

Get control of your past by reviewing and sharing your memories. Don't brood over it like the embers of a fire; rake it over and let the live coals come to the surface. And don't share your problems and burdens. Nobody wants to hear about those, since people have enough of their own. If they fail to respond to you because you're boring them with your troubles, that will only increase your feeling of isolation and make matters worse. Good memories make good conversation!

Deliberately, every day, reach back into your memory to review past blessings. Especially latch onto the times when all seemed hopeless and God snatched you from the brink of disaster. That kind of recall isn't living in the past as though the past were still the present; it's thinking back and giving thanks, receiving fresh impetus to face the challenges of today. Remember—the discipline of the memory honors God. It fosters the kind of thanksgiving He desires. It tones up your prayer life. It produces a winsome personality and encourages joy. And it helps you win over loneliness!

12

Set Your Sights

You've gotten right with your present and right with your past. Now get right with your future!

Let me return briefly to the analogy of the highway I used in the last chapter. We're all on life's road. And in a sense as Christians we're all going to the same place. But some of us are vague about the route we're taking. We don't use the map, but instead drift along with one hand on the wheel and the other hanging out the window, gazing vacantly at the horizon. We assume that keeping our foot on the accelerator is enough to get us where we're going.

That may be true, but I believe that God has some closer destinations He wants us to reach before we get to glory. Achieving those destinations should be a major priority for all of us. God hasn't only called you to salvation; He has also given you a unique purpose, a destination that you—and you only—are meant to reach. The highest end of your life as a Christian is to glorify God by finding that purpose and then optimizing its fulfillment.

Look at Paul. He said of his work as an apostle, "This one thing I do." Be honest: How many of us could say that? Most of us would have to admit, "These fifty things I dabble in!" Yet experience itself should teach us that dabbling merely frustrates us by multiplying the effort and diminishing the returns. What we need is a rigorous method of organizing the future so that when it becomes the present we know what we want to do with it. It's a technique that people have been talking about for a long time and not doing properly. It's called *goal-setting*.

Getting Ahead in the Goal Game

Christians can be particularly bad at goal-setting. Maybe that's because they see their lives as being controlled from the outside. Ask the typical Christian why he has no goals and he's likely to reply, "I'm waiting on the Lord." But as Dwight L. Moody once said, "It's all right to wait on the Lord as long as you hustle while you wait!"

Most of our limitations are not imposed on us by God—we impose them on ourselves. Loneliness encourages this effect. To a lonely person the future looks like a wasteland—miles of rough country that he's going to have to traverse on foot. If he's the Ugly Duckling, the prospect will stimulate his sense of inadequacy, and he will prefer to ignore the problem, diverting his attention to something else instead.

The goal-setter, however, sees much more than a wasteland. To his eye that stony terrain is crossed by a brand-new highway—all he has to do is get down and build it. Goal-setting is not just the opposite of the inertia produced by loneliness—it is a way of overcoming that inertia. It integrates the entire personality and makes for emotional wholeness. But it needs a kick start, and for that you'll want to cultivate two qualities.

First, *decisiveness*. Loneliness by its very nature deals with wisps, phantoms, unrealities, and speculations. For the lonely person, decision comes last on the list of priorities, because it orients the decision-maker toward one set of possibilities and cuts him off from all the rest. The Latin root of the word "decision" means precisely that—to cut off. *But decisiveness is vital.* You must focus your energies if you're going to get the future under control and win over loneliness.

My brother Ted had a terrible accident as a young man. It knocked one of his eyes askew. Day after day, in an attempt to treat him, the doctors had him look into something resembling an old stereopticon slide. He would look at the same image first with one eye and then with the other. Then he would open both eyes at the same time and, by turning little cranks, try to superimpose the images. He said it nearly knocked his head off because the pain was so unbearable. But he persevered because the doctors told him he would permanently damage his sight if he didn't, and today his vision is perfect.

Goal-setting is like getting both eyes in focus. Jesus stressed the importance of having a "single eye"—a single purpose, objective, or goal. That applies to the whole of life, not only the matter of commitment to Christ. James tells us that "a double-minded man is unstable in all his ways" (James 1:8). God doesn't want double-minded indecisive disciples; He wants dedicated men and women who pursue and achieve their objectives. Don't misunderstand me—I'm not advocating workaholism here. The workaholic depends on work to compensate for inadequacy in other areas of his life. But the goal-setter isn't running away from anything. He's taking control and making maximum use of his resources to cover the full range of his responsibilities. This means that, unlike the workaholic, he can put his business down at the end of the day and still be free from loneliness.

Second, goal-setting requires *discipline*.

It takes some courage to commit yourself to a goal. Doing so involves a certain finality, an awareness of responsibility, and a willingness to pass the point of no return. But once declared, a war must be waged to the end. There is no point in making a decision, setting a goal, and then chickening out because the going gets tough. Sure, there are risks—that's part of the deal. The battle to win over loneliness is no soft option. I warned you in Chapter 6 that you'd need discipline, and this is one place you need it!

It takes no discipline at all to sunbathe in self-pity, and very little discipline to tackle loneliness with the blockout and the facelift described in Chapter 4. Discipline isn't easy. But if the discipline involved in goal-setting is making you think twice, consider for a moment the reasons you don't want to take it on.

It could be that you're *afraid*. Forging a new way of life brings an encounter with the unknown. That can be scary. It's far more comfortable to repeat tomorrow what we've done today, no matter how miserable or dishonorable today's activities have been—better the devil you know than the devil you don't! But think: Isn't it better to have no "devil" at all?

You may be too *proud*. Nobody likes to admit he's been wrong, and a change in lifestyle implies that strongly. Loneliness in particular has such a stigma attached to it that you'd probably die before telling your friends about it. But at this point I have to ask you what you want. Do you want to shore up the feeble defenses of your own ego, or do you want freedom? Pride is a poor excuse for misery. In any case, your friends probably already know that you're lonely (they're probably lonely too). What do you have to lose?

Finally, you may be *lazy*. Yes, lazy. In adulthood many people develop a sort of mental inertia. They may not like loneliness, and they may not exactly be afraid of the new ideas and experiences that will help them win over it, but they're held back because they can't be bothered to make the effort. Misery isn't pleasant, but at least it's free. Well, once again: What do you want—ease or liberation? It's up to you. Remember that mental inertia isn't something that a goal-setter is stuck with for long. Once you get into goal-setting, your whole state of mind will change. It works like a vacation. Once taken outside its familiar routines your mind will become more elastic, more ready to respond with speed and accuracy, more like the mind of Christ. And the mind of Christ is alert, not atrophied; bright, not bored; creative, not constricted; dynamic, not dull; energetic, not enervated!

The Goal-Setters

Victory over loneliness is really just a side effect of goal-setting. That's as it should be, because loneliness itself is only a side-effect—that of a disorganized life. Put the life straight—get right with God, with yourself, with others—and the loneliness disappears. When you set your goals, therefore, you're not just adopting a strategy to counter a small emotional hang-up; you're revolutionizing your life.

History shows that people with well-defined goals are the ones who succeed. Years ago, Emory S. Bogardus said that what distinguishes achievers from nonachievers is "the focalization of psychic energy." In other words, the secret lies not in brains, charm, family, or background but in the ability to bring all your energies to bear on a single, sharply defined goal. Andrew Carnegie, the steel king, put the same idea in more practical language: "Put all your eggs in one basket and then watch that basket that nobody kicks it over."

Many of the great accomplishments of our society can be attributed to the dedicated goal-setting of one individual. You've seen Wedgwood pottery? It's world-famous. But did you know that the originator, Josiah Wedgwood, was born poor and physically handicapped? He lived in a dirty English industrial town called Burslem where workers got small wages and died young. But Josiah fell in love with a wealthy cousin, Sarah, and set about earning a dowry of several thousand pounds so that he could marry her.

For five years he worked in Sheffield, where he developed a reputation as an extraordinary potter. From there he wrote to Sarah of his future plans: "Burslem shall yet be a symbol of all that is beautiful, honest and true; and I'll be the best potter England has ever seen. . . ." Some goal to set himself! Yet four years after he had returned to his hometown he had earned more than enough for the dowry. He and Sarah were married. That goal reached, he made for the next, laboring with his wife to make Burslem an art center and the home of Queensware. In the end Josiah was appointed potter to the Queen and became the richest man of his day. He succeeded through goal-setting.

Another famous goal-setter was Thomas Edison. You'll be hard pressed to find another man so dedicated to his work. A well-known writer once asked Edison, "Is it true that you experimented 10,000 times with the electric light filament before you were successful?"

"That is true," Edison replied.

"How do you account for the fact that you succeeded on the ten thousandth experiment?"

"I exhausted the possibilities of failure."

"Suppose you had not succeeded the ten thousandth time. What would you have done?"

"I'd still be experimenting," said Edison, "instead of wasting my fool time talking to you about it!"

You may think I'm aiming a bit high when I illustrate the principle of goal-setting with such monumental figures as Wedgwood and Edison. Do I really expect my readers to achieve feats like theirs? Yes, I do. Of course not everyone has the potential to do exactly what they did. Your goal should be tailored to your personal abilities. If you're a typist, I wouldn't advise you to start setting your goals in the area of quantum physics.

But if your skills lie in an area more modest than advanced science or top-level government, this should not deter you from setting goals on the same scale. In God's power the greatest accomplishments are within your reach.

Let me tell you about Hattie Wiatt. She was just a little girl who lived at the latter end of the last century and worshiped with her family at the Grace Baptist Church, set up in 1880 in Philadelphia by the converted lawyer Dr. Russell Conwell. The church was only a ramshackle building. As the congregation grew, the day came when Hattie Wiatt couldn't even get in the doorway, so large were the crowds attending the service. She went home tearful, and told her mother that many of her friends had been unable to go to Sunday school. "Mama," she said, "we must have a bigger church."

A few weeks later Hattie Wiatt got sick. She had consumption, and in three months she was dead. Dr. Conwell gave the funeral address. But just as he was mounting the rostrum, Hattie's mother came forward with a small, shabby red purse in her hand and gave it to him.

Dr. Conwell opened the purse and found inside 57 pennies, with a note saying simply: "For our new church."

The preacher knew what sacrifice had gone into that gift. He also knew how wide a gulf was fixed between those 57 cents and the cost of a new church. But the goal that this small child had set was destined to go all the way to fulfillment. Dr. Conwell told the congregation about the gift, and the people were moved. They began to give in a way they had never done before. Men would walk home from work to put money aside. Four years later, by the sacrifice of those men and women, and by the vision given to them by the little girl, the congregation moved into the finest church building in the whole of America. It had better acoustics than the best music halls. It held 9000 worshipers at each of the three morning services. And on the very first Sunday it was debt-free!

The story doesn't stop there. Inspired by Hattie Wiatt, Russell Conwell put together that great oration "Acres of Diamonds." He preached it 6000 times and raised nine million dollars. With that money he was able to found Temple University and build the Good Samaritan Hospital—now the Temple University Hospital. A church, a university, and a hospital—all for 57 cents! Who could have guessed that the goal set by a six-year-old girl would stretch so far?

I can relate to Hattie's story because something similar has happened to me. As a boy of ten I committed my life to the work of the Lord in China. The war prevented me from following through on that goal in the way I originally thought, but though I changed my grip, I never changed my goal. And today through the Haggai Institute my boyhood dream is being realized. By the end of 1987, more than 5000 national leaders have trained an estimated 700,000 of their fellows for the Lord's work in over a hundred countries. Between them they're working with more Chinese than I would ever have reached as a missionary!

Goal-Setting: The Technique

Henry Kaiser's formula for goal-setting was to determine what you want more than anything else in life; to write it down in one sentence; to write down the means by which you intend to attain that goal; and finally to permit no one and nothing to deter you from achieving it.

I break down my approach into four stages:

1. *Establish goals and review them daily.* You're lucky—you live in an age when the diversity of possible goals is enormous. But that can lead to its own problems. For example,

you may be saying now, "But there are so *many* things I want to accomplish."

If that's so, be ruthless. You will have time to accomplish many short-term goals, but you won't have time for more than one big one. So take time to determine the one overriding purpose of your life. What is the one all-encompassing goal you want to realize?

I spent most of 1958 determining what my life goal would be. I went through I don't know how many yellow pads. Finally, in the fourth week of November, I came to a happy conclusion. Looking back now, that period was one of the most valuable investments of my life. It was a definite objective that sustained me in the difficult years that followed. On at least two occasions I seemed to be on the brink of disaster—it seemed the office doors were going to be padlocked and the organization forced to fold. But reference to my goal, and the assurance that God had directed me in its establishment, kept me moving forward and smiling.

It's important that your goal be creative. Let it be your own action under God. You are a distinct personality, with gifts, qualities, and insights that no one else possesses. Bring those divine gifts into play. It may be that you, like me, can make your major goal your life's work. That's great—a preacher can aim to perfect his preaching and an artist to impact his contemporary culture. But other options are open to you. You can pursue your goal not only in your work, or by doing your work in a certain way; you can pursue it *outside* your normal work. After all, Paul earned his living making tents, and his real goals had to be chased in his spare time. Remember that what begins as a spare-time occupation may grow to take up your entire day.

The important point is to determine your priority and focus on it. Daily review is advisable, as this lifts your spirit and keeps you in mind of your overall objectives. Do that, and you will find your life taking on a greater resilience and an attractive buoyancy. You probably won't have time to wallow in loneliness even if you felt the inclination, because your goal will make life exciting and challenging.

Even the most successful people can sometimes lose that sense of challenge. Look at John D. Rockefeller. By the time he reached his fifties he was sick with boredom. Then a minister suggested that he get involved with worthwhile projects, underwriting important programs that would honor God and bless mankind. He made that his goal. In the end he gave away 232 million dollars—probably over two billion in today's markets. He found a new dimension in life and lived well into his nineties.

2. *Set target times.* Goals that aren't tied down to a schedule tend not to be realized, so always give your goal a target time—a time when you expect to have done what you set out to do. But don't *only* set a target time. A big project will seem overwhelming unless you have some way of charting your progress. So split the work up into stages. Reaching intermediate targets will help to build your confidence and give you a sense of accomplishment.

Years ago, CBS commentator Eric Sevareid related the story of a long march he took part in during World War Two. He had loose hobnails in his boots. The trek was so long that the only way he could handle it was to think, literally, of one step at a time. The story was a parable for the rest of his life. If someone had told him, he said, how many words he would have to write in the following 25 years, he would have called it impossible. Yet by turning out one commentary at a time he was able to turn out enough copy to fill an encyclopedia.

In my younger days I developed the habit of memorizing the Scripture passages I used when I preached or taught Sunday school. Looked at in its entirety, a week's learning seemed beyond me. But if I divided the passage into six parts and learned one every day, I always managed to learn it all by Sunday. I can hardly put into words what benefits I gained from that practice. As a young preacher it firmed up my thinking and filled me with such enthusiasm that my hearers were moved by my spirit even if I failed to make my points clear in words!

Incidentally, that period of my life also illustrates the problems you can run into by relying on yourself instead of God.

In my first charge I was still struggling with feelings of extreme inadequacy. For the first two years I wanted to resign every Monday morning, so disconsolate was I with my performance the previous day! Lonely? I even felt isolated from myself. I went as far as questioning my call to the ministry and looking in the classified ads for another job.

But while reflecting one day I realized that all this was a trick of Satan. He is a master of discouragement. He hadn't gotten to me by attacking the ministry; he had simply dropped the suggestion that I wasn't worthy to fulfill it. And in that he was absolutely right: I wasn't worthy! Our sufficiency is of God. The fact that I felt I was making a hash of my calling was unimportant. God had still called me to it. It was His goal for me, and He was giving me His strength to achieve it. I was reviewing my weekly targets all right—the problem was that I paid undue attention to my own weakness, looking on myself as the Ugly Duckling and thereby growing discouraged. In the terminology of Chapter 6, I had learned discipline but not dependence.

Don't make the same mistake!

3. *Maintain a daily creative-action list.* This means breaking down your overall objective into smaller, short-term assignments. It's a marvelous antidote to loneliness because it concentrates your mind. When you've established your goal, break down the action required to achieve it into annual, monthly, weekly, and daily schedules. Even break down your days.

Planning like this will take time. Don't worry about that—a few days off to soberly and creatively lay out your course of action will be well invested. And don't feel that you have to stick to every detail of your original plan. Circumstances change, so make the plan flexible. Just as it's easier to steer a bike when it's moving, so it's often easier to do the fine-tuning on a creative-action list when the project is already going. Always look to God for guidance. Rely on the Holy Spirit, the Spirit of Truth, to spell out the plan. As the psalmist said: "The steps of a good man are ordered by the Lord."

You might also say that the *stops* of a good man are ordered by the Lord. So be prepared for God to make changes.

Organizing a daily creative-action list will confront you with the question of priorities. Since not all the elements of your life are of equal value, I suggest that you follow the recommendation of Alan Lakein, sometimes called "America's time czar." There's nothing hard about it. He says to identify your list of actions and then divide the components into three grades, labeling them A, B, and C. This will help you concentrate on the most important goals. If you want to, subdivide each group—A1, A2, A3, and so on. What you fail to get done in one day, defer to the next. It doesn't matter if you don't get through your whole list, but at least you'll know you've covered the priorities.

You may think a creative-action list is making a mountain out of a molehill. After all, isn't it a bit extreme to be so businesslike about minor matters? But think about this: None of us has more than 24 hours in a day. And in that 24 hours we all use roughly the same amount of time for sleeping, working, washing, dressing, eating, and praying. Add up the time spent doing those essential activities, subtract it from 24, and you get approximately two discretionary hours. When you realize that the difference between success and failure in life can be the way you use those two hours a day, the creative-action list suddenly becomes very important!

The creative-action list has another advantage too: It helps to counter feelings of inadequacy by making you feel good about your calling. By using it you begin to have a feeling that you're doing something worthwhile, something completely and uniquely yours. You are leaving the murky lowlands of loneliness and climbing to the Alpine peaks of adventuresome productivity. Your life has meaning, purpose, and dynamism. Defeats are no longer defeats—only temporary setbacks. You go sideways every now and then, but overall you're moving steadily upward.

4. *Make your runway 21 days long*. Many psychologists have concluded that three weeks is the minimum time required to

establish a new behavior pattern. So for the first 21 days at least you must be absolutely strict with yourself. Think of that 21 days as a runway without which you'll never get into the air.

Don't skip a day. I recommend that you set aside a sufficient period of time every Friday afternoon or sometime on Saturday to review the past week and prepare for the next. Revisions may be necessary. Make them, provided that they will strengthen you and speed your progress toward your goal. Then, every morning as you conclude your quiet time, review your goals, go over your creative-action list, and set your course for the coming day. If you can, take a moment or two at the end of the day—preferably at least an hour before you go to bed—to chart your progress and project your plans. In the end it will be worth your while to take one full day each month for review and planning. This may seem like a terrific waste of time, but I promise you that the more thorough your planning, the more joyous will be your results.

I suggest that you do not at any stage share your goal with other people. One reason is that talking about your goals gives you the same release as accomplishing them, and hence weakens your effort. A second reason is that other people who do not have goals will almost certainly discourage you. "Oh, I used to do that," they'll say, "but now I'm a realist." You can do without that kind of blow, so don't hang your chin out.

It doesn't matter, anyway, what others think. In John 21, where Jesus gives Peter a special commission, the first thing Peter does is look over his shoulder and ask, "And what shall this man do?" "What is that to thee?" Jesus replies; "Follow thou me." He is saying the same to you: "Follow thou me." In other words, don't try to find meaning in your life by referring to the experience of other people. You're a unique individual. There's no one else like you. You have abundant life in the power of God. And you have a special calling.

But finally, remember that your special calling is put in the context of another calling that is common to all Christians—

the ultimate goal of conformity to Christ. Nothing in your goal-setting should contradict or impede that most vital goal. Indeed, your overarching purpose, that of taking on the likeness of Christ, will give you strength and inspiration in the pursuit of your life goal: "Look unto Jesus. He is the author and finisher of our faith."

It's said that whenever President Teddy Roosevelt reached an impasse, and didn't know what to do, he would swivel around in his chair and look at the picture of Abraham Lincoln in his office. Then he would ask himself, "I wonder what *he* would do?" That often did the trick. The same is true for us, except that we are privileged to have not the picture of a dead president but the presence of the living God!

Part 4

GET RIGHT WITH OTHERS

13

The Basics

Getting right with others is what this whole book has been leading up to—it is the divine answer to loneliness. But if you've turned to this page right at the beginning, without reading the rest of the book, I warn you that it will do you no good. The formula for winning over loneliness is in three parts, and the last one rests on the other two just like a rider sits on a saddle, and the saddle sits on the horse. Have you ever tried riding with no saddle and no horse? Forget it—go back and start at the beginning!

For the rest of you, a chance to refresh your memory. The formula for your victory over loneliness looks like this:

> GET RIGHT WITH GOD
> GET RIGHT WITH YOURSELF
> GET RIGHT WITH OTHERS

Getting right with God starts with learning the thanksgiving habit, and moves on to establishing your quiet time and living in contentment. Getting right with yourself means getting right in all three tenses—present, past, and future: in other words, thought-control, memory-control, and goal-setting.

What have I been asking you to do in these first two stages? In essence I have been asking you to make those fundamental changes that will turn you into a person able to overcome loneliness. That's why those stages are so vital. Just as a stunt rider cannot do a death-defying leap over 20 buses without getting up the necessary acceleration, so it is impossible to win over loneliness without first getting right with yourself and with God. In all likelihood it is some problem in your relationship with God or your own self that has damaged your relationship with other people and made you lonely.

Now that you've arrived at the final stage, I want you to take stock. You've come a long way. You've climbed three-quarters of the mountain and you're ready to make the assault on the summit. It's advisable at this point to check that all your equipment is in order, and that you understand fully the nature of the task ahead of you. Making friends, like climbing mountain peaks, is an activity that demands correct attitude and technique. It is also one on which the Bible supplies some direct and unique teaching.

The Principle of Service

It is a common fault of human nature to look at relationships from the receiver's point of view.

Everybody wants "fulfillment," "satisfaction," "love," and "respect." Of course everyone agrees that there must be giving as well as taking, but the social transactions occurring between persons tend to mirror financial transactions between companies: The arrangement must be of mutual benefit or else one of the partners will soon want out. Giving is a price we pay in order to receive. The result is that relationships break down if one side makes demands which the other feels are unreasonably heavy, or if one side continues to ask for reasonable favors without reciprocating in kind. To take a random example: Sex used as an exchange of love is good and strengthens a marriage, but as soon as a husband requires his conjugal rights without showing love and respect for his wife, the relationship is damaged and the marriage put under strain.

In cases where relationships have already broken down, the desire to receive often comes to the fore. We've all met a wino who asks for money. If he's feeling bright he sometimes tries to engage you in conversation first; if he's not, he comes right out and asks for money. You are no longer another human being to him—merely a source of cash. Drink, of course, isn't the only problem that produces this kind of effect; there are many others. But one of them is loneliness. Have you ever noticed how being lonely makes you more demanding of other people—of their time, their attention, their generosity? It's not that you become totally selfish, but that the awareness of your own need which arises in loneliness makes it harder to achieve a proper balance of give-and-take which most people expect of you. You perhaps get a reputation for talking too much (demanding time) or of holding aloof (demanding respect).

The answer to this social effect of loneliness—which is the one you are probably most wanting to cure—lies clearly in Scripture. Look at Christ: Here was a Man surrounded with difficult people—sick people, hostile people, cynical people, ignorant people. Sometimes even His own disciples were more concerned about their status in heaven than the preaching of the gospel on earth. Yet He never showed signs of loneliness. Why not? I believe the answer is to be found in the way He approached others—a way that He laid down as a supreme principle of Christian discipleship.

Read the Gospels and you will see for yourself this remarkable fact about Jesus; He did not seek to receive from others.

> He that is greatest among you, let him be as the younger; and he that is chief, as he that doth serve. For which is greater, he that sitteth at meat or he that serveth? Is not he that sitteth at meat? But I am among you as one that serveth (Luke 22:26,27).

Ask yourself this question: Are you one who gets served, or one who serves? If you're one of the served, you're on dangerous ground. The reason is obvious. To be served is to depend on the willingness of others to serve you. You may have some kind of "greatness" that invites such service, but the service itself is beyond you, outside your control. And that makes you vulnerable. What happens when you get moved out of the limelight and into the lounge? No more media coverage. No more testimonial dinners. No preferential parking space or waiting limousine. No leaders standing in line to get a word of greeting or counsel. That fact is that this is where the served person often finishes his life—

washed up on the lonely shores of old age. Not many of his former admirers will follow him there. For the served person, a point always comes when service (in the form of praise, deference, attention, or obedience) can no longer be bought. Not even the wealthiest man can assure himself of being served to his death.

In contrast, the beautiful thing about serving is that you can continue unhindered to the end. Nobody is going to refuse your service if it is genuinely and discreetly offered. And you will never find yourself in a situation where service is impossible. Suppose you're laid up in the hospital with your leg in traction. You can still encourage other patients, be helpful to the nursing staff, or just give a smile. Such small acts of service—thoughtfulness, kindliness, gratitude—are enormously important because they make other people feel better. And this is beneficial for you, since it's usually the generous people who are the most popular. But don't make the mistake of serving others just to be popular. Jesus didn't say to serve those who thank you (anybody will do that—it's just the old custom of giving-to-receive-again); on the contrary, service is a principle to be followed impartially in even the hardest of circumstances:

> Ye have heard that it hath been said, "Thou shalt love thy neighbour and hate thine enemy." But I say unto you, "Love your enemies, bless them that curse you, do good to them that hate you, and pray for them which despitefully use you and persecute you. . . ."
>
> For if ye love them which love you, what reward have ye? Do not even the publicans the same? And if ye salute your brethren only, what do ye more than others? Do not even the publicans so? Be ye therefore perfect, even as your Father which is in heaven is perfect (Matthew 5:43,44,46,47).

Serving Your Generation

A splendid example of the life of service is provided for us in Scripture by David. What finer epitaph could a Christian hope for than the one given to this man by Paul in his sermon at Antioch of Pisidia:

> David, after he had served his own generation by the will of God, fell asleep, and was laid unto his fathers (Acts 13:36).

What can we learn from David?

First of all, that David served God in spite of his inadequacy. He wasn't born into the aristocracy. He didn't even have an education: He spent his youth as a little fellow looking after his father's livestock. But those years taught him an important lesson, and when he arrived at the Israelite camp on an errand from his father, and saw the warriors of Israel confronting the nine-foot giant Goliath with their Adam's apples pumping up and down like bubbles in a steam gauge, he put his feelings of inadequacy where they belonged.

The key verse is found in 1 Samuel 17:45. David hadn't received much encouragement. When he asked his older brothers why no one had taken up Goliath's challenge of single combat, they dismissed him as a nuisance and a troublemaker. King Saul—who hadn't exactly been deluged with offers—finally accepted David, but tried to compensate for David's weakness by giving him the royal suit of armor. David refused. He didn't want to fight in a sardine can. He didn't need armor because it wasn't David, with all his inadequacy, who was going to do the fighting. Listen to his response to Goliath's taunt:

> Then said David to the Philistine, "Thou comest to me with a sword, and with a spear, and with a shield, but I come to thee in the name of the Lord of hosts, the God of the armies of Israel, whom thou hast defied. This day will the Lord deliver thee into mine hand . . . for the battle is the Lord's, and he will give you into our hands" (1 Samuel 17:45-47).

You don't need me to tell you the rest of the story. If you don't know it already, look it up and read it! But note that

David was not afraid to use violence when violence was the only way to dethrone evil. And note particularly that he didn't let inadequacy slow him down. He knew that God had called him to this fight, and knew that on paper he shouldn't make it through the first round. You may be familiar with feelings like that. You may wish you had a better education, a sounder upbringing, a more distinguished background, a few more breaks. Take courage—service isn't about qualifications. Whatever the challenge you face, however big your Goliath, remember that one-plus-God is a majority.

"But what if I am unworthy?" you may ask. "What if there's been some bad scene in my life that neutralizes my service?"

That may be. In looking at your past you may well find a socially offensive defection, an "inexcusable" sin. You might have shared it with another person or kept it to yourself. But it has continued to gnaw at you, sucking the vitality from your joy and paralyzing your freedom.

Golden rule number one: Never wink at sin. It's serious, and it has to be dealt with.

But there's more to it than that. Golden rule number two: Never doubt God's forgiveness. First John 1:9 makes it absolutely clear that forgiveness is available for every child of God: "If we confess our sins, he is faithful and just to forgive us our sins, and to cleanse us from all unrighteousness." You must not try to share the glory of God by setting yourself up as your own judge and executioner! God alone has the privilege of judgment, and if He has promised you complete forgiveness of your sin through the blood of Jesus Christ when you truly confess and repent, that is the end of the matter. Your record is wiped clean.

If you don't believe that, look again at David. I tell you, if you read the two books of Samuel you'll find plenty of bad scenes in David's life. At one point he committed adultery and then killed the woman's husband. You might wonder how David, the man of God who succeeded Saul as king of Israel, could ever have done such a thing. We always expect

God's servants to be irreproachable! But wait a minute. Anyone demanding perfection from others has never examined the depths of his own heart. I have yet to discover a person who hasn't at one time or another harbored a desire that, carried to its conclusion, would land him in the penitentiary for life. Many times over the years I've challenged audiences to find someone. Nobody ever has!

David stumbled badly, and everybody knew it. Yet after he had been restored he continued to serve God with great effectiveness. Ironically, his sin opened up a new opportunity for service through witnessing to the grace of God. In the penitential psalm written after the episode of adultery with Bathsheba we read: "Then will I teach transgressors thy ways, and sinners shall be converted unto thee" (Psalm 51:13). If God could wipe out the stains for David, He can do the same for you.

Not that David's life was easy. Service never is. After he slew Goliath, David was able to expand the sphere of his service from shepherding on the hills to leading the armies of Israel. But that same expansion came laden with the jealousy of Saul. In the years that followed, David many times came within a whisker of death, yet he continued to serve God and, as far as he was able, to serve the king. Many times he could have acted as the "receiver" and not as the "giver." Had he heeded his friends' advice to kill Saul, for example, the kingdom would have fallen into his hands, and the armies of Israel, ordered by Saul to kill him, would at once have submitted to his command. The king had unwittingly gone alone into the very cave where David and his men were hiding. Yet David refused to take what God had not yet given him:

> He said unto his men, "The Lord forbid that I should do this thing unto my master, the Lord's anointed. . . ."
> Saul rose up out of the cave and went on his way. David also arose afterward, and went out of the cave and cried after Saul, saying, "My lord the

king!" And when Saul looked behind him, David stooped with his face to the earth and bowed himself (1 Samuel 24:6-8).

Firm obedience in moments of such temptation is hard. But it is part of service to serve others even when they take it for granted or outrightly rebuke you. That's giving away your cloak and going the extra mile. And life presents us with many opportunities to put Jesus' teaching to the test. You may well find your greatest opposition coming from your own group, your own church, even your own family. John Wesley's wife nefariously secured some intimate letters, had them doctored to make him appear in the worst possible light, and then circulated them among his enemies. A lesser man would have despaired and given up his ministry. But under God, John Wesley strode on and probably had a greater impact on his generation than any other Christian in the English-speaking world. Remember: If you're doing something good, you'll always meet opposition. There's no motion without friction, no service without resistance. David's life sets an example in many other areas of service.

He served God in his natural abilities—in dance, music, and song. You may be able to serve in that way too. Or perhaps you have another, different talent?

David served God with his finances. For the construction of the temple eventually carried out by his son Solomon, he made a personal gift amounting in modern currency to more than 200 million dollars. You may not have money like that to give away, but you'll have *some*. Did you know that in Old Testament times the Israelites gave away more than 23 percent of their income? In America, a glorious land of freedom and material blessing, Christians average about 2.5 percent. Are you impoverished by your stinginess?

Finally, David served God in prayer. This is hardly the least important area of service, even if it does come last! But it is the most versatile. If you have no chances to use your talents, and no money to give away, you can still serve God by praying.

Aren't you encouraged when someone says to you, "I've been praying for you"? Doesn't that lift your spirits? Of course it does. And prayer does more, both for the person prayed for and the person praying, than either one can imagine, because it brings them both to the very throne of grace.

By the Will of God

David's life provides us with inspiration for the life walked in the footsteps of Christ, the life of service. But keep in mind what Paul said of David—that he served his own generation by the will of God.

On the one hand this suggests the comprehensiveness of Christian service. Serving isn't something you do in the moments left over when you've finished your work and your goal-setting. Service is an ethos which permeates every aspect of life, from the casual contacts you make on your travels to the pursuit of your life goal. You live to serve God, and serving God means serving other people. To be a Christian is to be a self-giving person.

On the other hand, Paul's phrase suggests the particularity of your service. The friends you make, the opportunities you have, and the goals you set are a way of service *special to you*. David had his unique calling, and you have yours. But you are still serving your generation by the will of God. God is still with you, as He was with David and with Joshua. Remember that promise? I WILL BE WITH YOU; I WILL NOT FAIL YOU OR FORSAKE YOU. As you move out of your old ways, seek God's presence, know that He is with you, and discover in the principle of service a full new life!

Such is the impression that Paul leaves us with—that David enjoyed life at its best. Service has that effect. There's no better way of getting into a church fellowship than offering to help with the washing up after coffee on Sunday morning. There's no easier way to feel the gratification of human contact than giving it to someone else—for example, by visiting hospital patients or prisoners. Serving puts you in the very image of Christ. It is a secret passageway leading to abundant life. If you begin your drive to get right with others by observing the principle of service, your lonely days are numbered. Loneliness cannot coexist with a full life lived in the power of God. You'll win over it forever!

14

Show Yourself Friendly

On one of my flights to Florida, a lovely young lady 22 years old was sitting next to me. I learned that she was a stewardess flying to Florida to visit an aunt who had suffered a severe personal loss.

It didn't take me 15 minutes to find out she was a committed Christian. She and her family worshiped at a lively church in Jackson, Mississippi.

I asked about her career.

"I heard stories about the behavior of some stewardesses, and even worse ones about some of the cockpit personnel. I knew if there were any truth to those stories, this job would either make me or break me as a Christian."

It was obvious the job was making her. She had turned out to be a radiant Christian with an infectious personality. The loneliness of her job—isolated from her family, living alone in a distant city, and spending hours at layover stops—did not drive her to attend parties or functions she knew would be inconsistent with her commitment to Christ. Loneliness had no hold on her. She had learned the secret of "getting right with others."

Not all relationships are good ones. That's why loneliness is often found *within* relationships. The lonely person isn't always the one with no personal contacts. He may be a renowned socialite, yet suffer the ravages of loneliness because all his contacts are inadequate. Loneliness results not just from an inability to form relationships, but from an inability to form relationships *of the right kind*.

Take the story of the prodigal son. None of those who gathered around him in his spendthrift days could rightly be called a "friend." No doubt he would have used that word, and thought they were all having a great time. But real friends don't desert you when the money runs out. They don't pay attention to you just because they want something from you—your time, your cash, your support, or your sexual favors. Real friends aren't receivers but givers.

That much is more or less common sense, for as the proverb says, "A friend in need is a friend indeed." But how do you tackle the problem of making good relationships? How do you get enough confidence to form real friendships, and not need to surround yourself with fair-weather friends and hangers-on?

Well, there is an art to it. It amazes me how haphazard many people are in the matter of friendship. They seem to think it's accidental. They are unaware of the scriptural principles that govern the formation and dispersion of friendships. Such principles are analogous to those used by an artist in painting portraits or a poet in writing sonnets. Observe them and the result is beautiful and pleasing; ignore them and it will probably be worthless.

The teaching of the Bible on friendship is neatly summarized right in the middle, in the book of Proverbs. There Solomon gives us this advice:

> A man that hath friends must show himself friendly, and there is a friend that sticketh closer than a brother (Proverbs 18:24).

In today's language we might render it like this: *If you want a friend, be one!*

Friendship is a reciprocal affair. Put yourself in the shoes of the people you meet: They probably don't want a bad relationship any more than you do. They want to be fed, built up, encouraged, consoled, made happy—just like you. There's not much you can do to influence their behavior toward you, and that's as it should be, for real friendship can only occur if both parties are free to choose. But if you want to attract and keep good friends, you do have one powerful factor under your control: yourself. Ask yourself, "Am I the kind of person I would like as a friend?" If you're not, do a little thinking about the reasons for your answer. To know that you are a "befriendable" person is important for your own confidence as well as for those who are going to be your friends!

What "showing yourself friendly" means in detail I have broken down into eight categories. I advise you to read them carefully, and test yourself on each one. What we're talking about here is the "you" that other people are relating to, the kind of person who will make a good friend.

Eight Features of Friendship

1. *Be real.* Most people have a "public image," a slightly improved version of themselves that they adopt to impress the world outside. For the Top Dog such an image constitutes a particular problem, because other people tend to relate to the image and not to the real person. The performer, for example, is expected to behave in private as he does on stage. But this problem of unreality, which all lonely people face, doesn't rest only on the false expectations of other people. It is a great temptation to hide behind your image all the time, because you know it can be relied upon to bring you respect. A minister, for example, may actually invite other people to treat him distantly by playing the role of a minister even when he is at home or on vacation.

No one can befriend your "public image." To have real friendship you must expose the real you. Not the high-flier, not the bright, young, health-conscious, omnicompetent businessman, not the capable attractive housewife and mother-of-three—just you. Maybe you think the "you" underneath the image isn't terribly impressive. But look at it from the other side. Have you ever thought how intimidating it is to other people to be confronted with someone who seems so perfect he would make Michael the archangel look shabby? What makes you feel secure can make others feel small!

You don't want that. You want to come across as warm and genuine. The English Puritan Oliver Cromwell was so insistent that people should see him as he really was that he told his portrait artist to leave in the warts. We all have warts of some sort or another. They help others to see we're really human, so don't paint them out!

It may be you're lucky enough not to have a well-developed public image. If so, don't try to acquire one. There's no need for drama in friendship, no need for affectation. Role-playing and pretended rapport with relative strangers will tend to embarrass others and increase your isolation. There are enough latter-day Judases around, with false smiles plastered over their faces, without your adding to their number.

2. *Be realistic.* Almost as big a mistake as presenting your own public image to others is expecting them to present theirs to you.

In layman's language this simply means: Don't have unreasonable expectations. You know about your own warts, so don't be surprised to find a few on other people. Remember that a friend will always let you down at some time or other, just as you will let him down. That's the imperfection of being human. The important point is not to let those incidents break your stride. As a "giver" in a relationship you are responsible for helping a friend through his problems and discouragements.

There are any number of simple ways to keep on affirming friendship and concern. God gave you muscles at the side of your mouth—use them to pull it out toward your ears in a smile! Take care to remember what others have said to you. And always be ready with a greeting. Have you noticed how God arranged the head so it's easier to nod it than wag it? Swinging your head from side to side to show disagreement or displeasure is real hard work. Yet to drop the chin in recognition or greeting takes so little effort that you can do it all day, every day, without the slightest fatigue.

The same with shaking hands. Think how difficult handshaking would be if God had put our knuckles the other way round! But as it is, two sets of fingers will fit around each other snugly, and the thumbs will fall on the other side to give a good, firm grip. Have a look at your right hand now. Is there a raw herring stuck onto the end of your arm? No? And what about the knuckles—are they facing the right way? Good—then make use of the hand that God has given you!

It's a great help to start your day by stocking up with kind thoughts, kind expressions, and kind greetings. Think of Psalm 118:24—"This is the day which the Lord hath made; we will rejoice and be glad in it." Determine that if someone does well you're going to say so, and that when someone looks better than he did the day before you're going to smile and say, "You're looking good today!" Even prepare to use silence properly. In some cases, a friend who is looking worn-out under the stresses and strains of life may take great consolation from the fact that you didn't seem to notice it.

3. *Be affirmative.* The same rule that covers your greetings extends to conversation in general. Think carefully about what you say in the company of other people, because things you say and the way that you say them have an enormous effect on your listeners. Remember the Smith Effect I talked about earlier. Gloomy words spread gloom. Of course there will be times when you need to get something off your chest, but there's a difference between a passing shower and interminable rain. So avoid as much as you can subjects such as your bad leg, the neighbor who's got it in for you, your dog that died, how terribly things are bound to turn out, and why you can't afford to take a vacation.

Cultivate a positive attitude to your life, and share your pleasures with others. There's nothing better than being uplifted by a talk with a friend. So if you're a friend, look for ways that you can uplift and encourage. Make others feel good about themselves. I don't mean that you should resort to abject flattery; complimenting a dowdily dressed lady on her attire is obviously insincere. But go out of your way to compliment anything about another person that deserves to be complimented.

A father once asked his little daughter, "Mary, why is it that everybody loves you?"

"I don't know," the girl replied, "unless it's because I love everybody."

4. *Be available.* Western society is ruled by the clock. That's fine for business, since scheduling appointments is only a way of using time to the best advantage. But it's important to remember that intensive time-scheduling of the kind you encounter in the business world tends to lay stress on the objective being pursued and not on the human relationships that surround it. Hence the prevalence of Top Dog loneliness in the executive class and even among church leaders.

If friendship matters to you (and if you are a Christian, friendship as well as family *ought* to matter to you), then it is necessary to give it time. "But I'm so busy," you may say, "and my work is so important." Of course it's important. If you've been getting right with your future by goal-setting, your work will have a key place in your life-goal. But God never calls anyone to be a monomaniac. Single-minded devotion to your goal is fine; single-minded refusal to pay attention to anything else is disobedience to God and spells ruination for your social life.

Your family and friends must have space in your diary. And by that I don't just mean chronological time: You probably spend eight hours a day in the same bed as your spouse, but that's not going far toward meeting either of your social needs. I'm talking about quality time, priority time, putting-others-first time. So schedule time to "waste" an afternoon playing football with the kids, browsing around a shopping mall with your wife, taking a walk, or seeing a movie with a friend. Giving good time to relationships is like putting good fertilizer on a plant: It produces growth. And that's what you want if you're going to win over loneliness.

5. *Be balanced.* I've just recommended balance in your use of time. But it is equally important to be balanced in your *activities*.

This is so because, as C.S. Lewis said in *The Four Loves*, friendship (unlike romantic love or simple acquaintance) arises from shared interest. A man and a woman who are in love stand, as it were, face-to-face, absorbed in each other. But friends stand side by side; their interest is taken up by some activity or pursuit that stands outside their own relationship. In fact we all know this from our own experience. We tend to have friends "at work" or "in church" or "at the club." Friends do not dwell on their friendship; it just flourishes because they are interested and excited by the same things.

It follows from this that a person seeking friendship must have interests over which friendship may form. Work doesn't wholly fit the bill here. Work throws us together with other people, but it doesn't always engage our interest, and in any case talking about work after hours is really allowing it to invade the privacy of our leisure. Much sounder advice to the lonely person is to take up a shareable hobby. Maybe you've always had a yen to go skydiving. Why not try it now? If you don't fancy jumping out of airplanes, there are plenty of more-sedate activities! It doesn't much matter what you do, provided that you like it and that it brings you in contact with other people who feel the same way.

6. *Be sensitive.* Lonely people easily forget that friendship has an etiquette. This isn't about the way you lay out soup spoons at the dinner table—unless, of course, you move in circles where misplacing soup spoons is liable to cause offense. It has to do with being polite and being sensitive to other people's needs. Everybody likes to be thanked for buying a meal or helping with the kids. Making your gratitude clear is courteous, pleasing to the friend, and stimulating for the friendship. Sending a birthday card is a practical way of demonstrating your appreciation for another person. So is keeping an eye out to make sure you're not outstaying your welcome when he or she has to be up early the next morning. Be sensitive to another person's needs even as you would want him or her to be sensitive to yours.

I remember participating in the same set of meetings as the late Pierce Harris in Jasper, Alabama. By then he was in his seventies. He had every right to retire after his early-morning lecture, but at my slot, every day at noon, he was always sitting in the audience. Many men of his age and experience would have taken the attitude: "This young whippersnapper has nothing to teach me. What does he know that I haven't already forgotten?" Yet he sat there, smiling and nodding, to encourage a young minister. I assure you he made a new friend that week!

7. *Be persistent.* As I've said before, it was Pierce Harris's habit to make three new friends every day. Friendship was an art he spent his life perfecting.

My father has done the same. As I write this book Dad is in his ninetieth year, but he still sticks to his regimen of making new contacts and maintaining old ones. He's a man who has been dedicated to his life goal—in fact he's just finished reading the Bible through for the 102nd time—but he's no monomaniac. He played tennis until the doctor ordered him to stop in his mid-eighties. Recently, when the teenagers of his church went away on a retreat, they insisted that he go along with them.

There's no chance of staying lonely once you've gotten into the habit of being a friend. People seek you out.

8. *Be a friend.* Being a friend of God helps you be a friend of man, and being a friend of man makes you a friend of God.

How we treat other people is the ultimate test of the way we treat our Lord. In the lesson on the sheep and the goats given to us in Matthew 25:31-46, Jesus makes it clear that good deeds done to our fellowmen are good deeds done to Him: "Inasmuch as ye have done it unto one of the least of these my brethren, ye have done it unto me" (Matthew 25:40). To imitate the friendship of the Good Samaritan is to imitate Christ Himself.

But we are not just friends of God through our obedience to His laws. To be a Christian is to know God in person. The grandest, mightiest, and tenderest friendship in all the universe is that between the Lord Jesus Christ and the believing soul. When the great New England preacher Jonathan Edwards had bid farewell to all his earthly friends, he turned on his pillow, closed his eyes, and asked, "Now, where is Jesus of Nazareth, my true and never-failing Friend?"

That relationship is the source of inspiration for all our human friendships. James talks about the wisdom of God, a wisdom that is freely available to God's children and encapsulates the spirit of genuine friendliness:

> The wisdom that comes from heaven is first of all pure and full of quiet gentleness. Then it is peace-loving and courteous. It allows discussion and is willing to yield to others; it is full of mercy and good deeds. It is wholehearted and straightforward and sincere (James 3:17 TLB).

Can you ask for a more perfect summary of what you want to be as a Christian friend? That is loneliness won over for good. And in the friendship of Jesus Christ it is yours for the asking.

15

Don't Slow Down

Get right with God, get right with yourself, get right with others. Follow that progression and you will have victory over loneliness. You'll have it licked, not just today and tomorrow, but every day for the rest of your life.

But I must emphasize: adopting a new lifestyle isn't like buying a refrigerator: You don't make a one-time payment, then sit back and forget it. You must go on applying what you've learned. Of course as time passes, winning over loneliness will get easier because your new lifestyle will become more natural to you. But don't let your foot off that accelerator. Don't slow down!

Some people who read this book may be saying, "That's all very well, but surely there comes a time in life when slowing down cannot be avoided—when it's too late to change your way of living and too hard to keep loneliness at bay."

I can only say that to me as a man of 64 that's nonsense. I tell you frankly that if Christ does not come in the meantime or take me to heaven, I still expect the best years of my life to be ahead. Why? Because the experience of countless others has proved to me that there is no reason for people over 60 to feel antiquated and useless. Thankfully, our leadership has raised the mandatory retirement age from 65 to 70, but isn't even 70 an arbitrary figure? I can think of men over 80 whose intellect, maturity, and zest for life more than qualify them for full-time employment. And if that's true, there's no reason for older people to be victims of loneliness any more than the young.

Maturity Rediscovered

Let me give you a few examples of achievement in later years.

Ever heard of Winston Churchill? Of course you have. But you probably wouldn't have if Churchill had died at 60. He was 65 at the outbreak of the Second World War. At a time of life when most people are winding down he was climbing the highest rung of the political ladder to lead Britain against the Nazis. Though he suffered a disastrous defeat in the postwar general election, he once again led his party to victory in 1951, and went on to serve as Prime Minister and Minister of Defence. He was 81 when he finally retired from politics. He died ten years later, a Nobel Prize winner and the author of a six-volume history of the Second World War.

Churchill could have slipped into obscurity in the late thirties. He could have won the war and then been embittered by his rejection at the polls. He could have soliloquized: "I gave my best, my very life, to these people. I deprived my family of normal companionship in order to spend endless hours conducting the war effort, so that Britain rose victorious from the very jaws of defeat. Now they've turned me out of office. Most of my closest friends are gone, and here I am, alone and unappreciated."

Not Churchill. Self-pitying loneliness wasn't his style. He didn't slow down, and by pursuing his life's goal to the end he stayed active and productive.

He's not the exception, either.

Benjamin Franklin was 70 years of age when he helped to draw up the Declaration of Independence, and 78 when he secured that independence as a cosignatory of the Treaty of Versailles. At 84, two years before his death, he was sitting on the convention that drafted the American Constitution.

At the same age John Knox, the great Scots reformer, was said to preach as well as he had ever done. John Wesley went on evangelizing into his eighties, and J. C. Massee into his nineties. Gladstone was in No. 10 Downing Street at 83. Both Bismarck and Crispi were in their mid-seventies when they occupied the top positions respectively in Germany and Italy. Dante did his best work in his sixties. The famous Boston cardiologist Paul Dudley White achieved greater international prominence in his eighties than ever before.

It is simply untrue that advanced years in themselves prevent a person from serving effectively. If you live long enough, being an octogenarian is something that will come to you as a matter of course. But being *ineffective* will come only if you let it. The same is true of loneliness.

Look at Herbert Hoover. This man had every reason to feel lonely. He was an idealist and humanitarian whose rise to the presidency coincided with the Wall Street crash of 1929 and the ensuing depression. When he was put out of office in 1932 he was accused of pigheadedness and of misrepresenting the facts to the American people. His name was invoked derisively as late as the fifties. Yet Hoover did not allow this loneliness to devastate him. He continued to regard himself as a servant of mankind, and served as chairman of the U. S. Commission of European Relief after the Second World War.

Another example is Harry Truman, who took over in the White House just in time to make that crucial decision on America's use of the atomic bomb in Japan. Up to that point he had suffered some extraordinary reverses, among them a failure in business which—because he insisted on paying his creditors in full—took him 15 years to put right. He became president at 60. He was maligned and belittled, and accused of cronyism with known gangsters. Yet he carried on to win a further term of office in 1948 and went on to encourage the formation of NATO and a policy of containment of Communism in Europe that became known as the "Truman Doctrine."

I do not quote the achievements of these men to make a political point. My intention is simply to show that neither was a candidate for loneliness. Both Hoover and Truman gained momentum when they were past 60.

A little while ago I heard Bob Hope's son interviewed on a TV program. I don't think there's much doubt that Bob Hope, who for many years has been the uncrowned king of American comedy, could have retired long ago with everything he ever wanted. But he pushes himself. At 75 he was maintaining a schedule that would have been tough for a man half his age. Yet it is often and erroneously believed that this familiar entertainer had it easy from the beginning. His son's comment was along these lines: "What people don't understand is that my father was about 40 years of age before his career got off the ground." Bob Hope was a late starter—and he's still going!

How to Stay Off the Shelf

Vigorous later years are a scriptural principle.

Moses reached 80 before he took up the leadership of Israel. Caleb, one of the spies he sent into the Promised Land with Joshua, was 85 by the time he finally received his inheritance. Caleb's testimony is an ideal to which all God's people should aim:

> Forty years old was I when Moses the servant of the Lord sent me from Kadesh-barnea to spy out the land. . . . And now behold, the Lord hath kept me alive, as he said, these forty-five years, even since the Lord spoke this word unto Moses, while the children of Israel wandered in the wilderness; and now, lo, I am this day eighty-five years old. As yet I am as strong this day as I was in the day that Moses sent me; as my strength was then, even so is my strength now, for war, both to go out and to come in. Now therefore give me this mountain (Joshua 14:7,10-12).

Caleb was claiming his possession at an age when most men would be superannuated and living with relatives. Yet the mountain of which he spoke was an area as yet unclaimed by the Israelites and occupied by the Anakims, some of the fiercest of the Canaanite tribes. Some job to take on at retirement! Yet Caleb relished the task because Moses had promised him this land as a reward for his faithfulness. He never lost sight of his life goal, and at 85 he was still striving to see it accomplished.

Caleb got his mountain: "Hebron therefore became the inheritance of Caleb . . . because he wholly followed the Lord God of Israel" (Joshua 14:14). If you continue to pursue your goals God will certainly give you your "mountain," whatever that is. It's not in God's plan for you to vegetate after a crucial turning point in your life—after the kids leave home or after you leave your job. There's no reason for any age to mark the peak of your life. God doesn't want you on the shelf at 60, 70, 80, or 90—so make sure you're not sitting on it!

Maybe that seems a little optimistic to you. After all, the human body does start to wear out. Physical disabilities accumulate, and restrictions on mobility tend to reduce a person's opportunities for social contact. Well, let me say that I'm aware of the privations of old age. We're not often like Caleb at 85, "as strong this day as I was." In countries like Britain, where extended family structures have broken down, the older person can literally be the Outsider, seldom visited and spinning out a meager existence in a cold, damp house with only memories for comfort.

I want to say something about people in such situations in the Epilogue. Here I will point out that to a very large extent, especially for the elderly in a wealthy nation like America, old age is what you make it. Sure, it imposes conditions that can lead to loneliness. But life can do that to you at any stage. Old age doesn't automatically bring defeat.

Let me introduce you to an old friend of mine whom I phoned this afternoon, Mrs. A. R. Almon. You would be hard-pressed to find someone more restricted than she is. She's 95. Her husband passed away years ago. Because she has arthritis she is unable to move about on her own. She can't read the Bible—or anything else—because she's blind. She can't even see television. She is completely housebound.

I asked her if she ever felt lonely. Yes, she said, there were times she felt lonely, but she felt no lonelier now than she did when she was in full health. She rejoiced that two of her close friends, now in their seventies, occasionally came to visit her, and said she found great companionship in her nurses. "I'll tell you, Dr. Haggai," she said, "as long as you are in a human body, you have periods of feeling one way and periods of feeling another. The Lord is always there, and all I need to do is reach out. His permanent presence is a wonderful comfort to me."

What is Mrs. Almon's secret? Simply that she has taken God's promise to heart. She knows that the Lord will never leave her or forsake her, and even though she is affected by the pain of loneliness, she is given the strength to win over it. In my estimation that qualifies her for a place alongside Herbert Hoover and Harry Truman, for gaining momentum after 60.

So if you feel you're on the shelf, start by asking yourself: "Am I on the shelf because God put me there, or because I put myself there?" If you think it's God's fault, think again. Of course your activities and your goals will change as you get older, but your opportunity to be effective for God will always be wide open. You never retire from life in Christ. Drawing your pension doesn't exempt you from the responsibility to improve your vitality and commitment, or to pass on the wisdom you've gained. If you're still alive, God's got work for you to do!

Here are a few suggestions to get you moving.

1. *Review your spiritual program.* It's the easiest thing in the world to grow complacent as you get older. At evangelistic meetings I am always struck by the disproportionate number of young people answering an invitation to surrender their lives or undertake some new spiritual responsibility. Do older Christians not need recommitment? Maybe they do but they're too proud to admit it!

In the wine trade older nearly always means better, but it's not always so with Christian faith. Tradition has it that Peter was the oldest of the disciples, yet was it not he who denied Christ during the trial. Or think of David, a monarch and a grandfather, committing adultery with Bathsheba and sending her husband Uriah to certain death. Abraham was no stripling when he jeopardized Sarah's purity by telling Pharaoh she was his sister. And as for Noah—wouldn't the man have more sense at 500 years than to get rolling drunk?

It's so easy to delude ourselves that we've grown in grace when we've grown only in knowledge. So I advise you to start by looking carefully at your commitment to God. Think about what you give to Him—how you use the first day of the week, and what you put in the collection. That may be only a starting point, but it will tell you a lot!

2. *Review your physical program.* First, get a checkup. There's nothing more infantile than avoiding a checkup just in case there's something wrong with you. If you're in good shape, there's nothing to worry about, but if you've got a serious illness like cancer, you'll live longer if you catch it early.

Second, think what's going to be on your plate at dinner tonight. Is it good for you, or is it going to put another inch on your waistline and a strain on your heart? Are you getting a good balance of the necessary foods? Make sure you're taking the right nutrition, in the right quantities, at the right time.

Third, if you don't have a regular exercise program, talk with your doctor about it and then adopt one. Be realistic—those 18 holes of golf aren't going to do much for you if you ride around in a golf cart! Walking is good exercise, and not dangerous. Jogging is best done under supervision, so don't expect to take up where you left off 30 years ago. Your body is probably capable of more than you realize (my friend the late E. Stanley Jones walked up to ten miles a day in his eighties), but if you're out of practice you'll need to ease in gradually.

3. *Review your intellectual program.* It's a good idea to have a specific reading discipline. Obviously this must start with Scripture, ideally early every morning. But on top of that, ask yourself what determines your choice of reading. Do you think out your choice, or is it made for you by *Time* magazine's best-seller list? Also, make sure you're using your memory. Learn some poetry, or Scripture verses, or useful data. If you've got a little time you might think of taking a speed-reading course to put zest into your intellectual program.

4. *Review your social program*. Start off by charting your progress in those positive habits that help win over loneliness. Are you still making thanksgiving a pattern in your life? Are you controlling your thoughts? Is your expression happy or sad, your walk energetic or fatigued, your thought pattern problem-oriented or opportunity-oriented?

Then go on to look at your social habits. Are you still making new friends and keeping old friendships in good repair? How generous are you with your friends? Do you introduce them to one another? Are you prompt in correspondence? Can you be relied on to remember birthdays, anniversaries, and special seasons? What about jumping in the car and arriving unannounced to let someone know you're hungry for fellowship? Make a long-distance call to someone who hasn't heard from you for a while, or send flowers to a person who's well, instead of waiting until he's sick or dead!

5. *Review your volitional program*. Do you always keep the vows you make to yourself? It's easy to overlook them when nobody else is looking. But that introduces an insidious weakness into your character. As Ecclesiastes says, "Better is it that thou shouldest not vow than that thou shouldest vow and not pay" (Ecclesiastes 5:5).

So when you make a commitment—even to yourself—make sure you count the cost. Determine whether or not you're willing to pay the price, and whether you'll still be willing five years from now. Remember, integrity is carrying out a commitment after the environment in which the commitment was made has dissipated. Do you have that kind of integrity?

If you do, you'll still be winning over loneliness.

16

Epilogue

There is nothing more exhilarating than personal victory through Christ in any area of life.

In winning over loneliness you will experience that victory. With Paul you will be able to say that you are "more than a conqueror":

> I am persuaded that neither death, nor life, nor angels, nor principalities, nor powers, nor things present, nor things to come, nor height, nor depth, nor any other creature shall be able to separate us from the love of God, which is in Christ Jesus our Lord (Romans 8:38-39).

Remember the promise which God gave to Joshua, which is yours as well? I WILL BE WITH YOU; I WILL NOT FAIL YOU OR FORSAKE YOU. Why can God never fail you or forsake you? Because in Christ nothing can separate you from Him: "Nor things present nor things to come," writes Paul. That includes the loneliness you experience in your present situation, and all the loneliness you will ever feel. No longer does loneliness have to cloud your personality, curtail your potential, or mar your effectiveness for God.

Get right with God, with yourself, and with others—and victory is yours!

If you have applied the truths of this book, and not just read through its pages, you will have embarked upon a new and victorious dimension of living. This new lifestyle will be filled with thanksgiving, service, love for other people, and above all a close companionship with the Lord Jesus Christ. Let that relationship be the root and source of your contentment.

Of course there will always be times of trial and hardship, of temptation and difficulty. God roughens the path here and there so that you will take hold of His hand. But that is no reason to be discouraged. It is said that the martyr John Noyra, in the midst of the flames that were consuming him, reached down to kiss a burning stick. "Blessed be God," he cried, "for the time when I was born for this preferment!" If he could bless God for a mercy as hard as that, surely we can do the same in our difficulties. For God has promised to be with us, and in His presence "the sufferings of this present time are not worthy to be compared with the glory which shall be revealed in us" (Romans 8:18).

But a word of caution: There is a danger that in tackling loneliness you will become too much concerned with *yourself*. You may be a lonely person, and you have every right as a child of God to win over that loneliness, but don't forget the other people whose loneliness may be far more acute than yours. Would you want to enjoy all the blessings of God's companionship while another person—for example, the elderly person I mentioned in the last chapter—is left overwhelmed by solitude? I don't think you would. And I would be contradicting the Word of God if I advised you to, for Paul said to the Galatians, "Bear ye one another's burdens, and so fulfill the law of Christ" (Galatians 6:2).

So I will leave you with a piece of simple, practical advice. If loneliness is your problem, make it a priority in your Christian service to start solving loneliness for somebody else. You will certainly find someone in your circle of acquaintances who needs your friendship. Put yourself out for this person, not in an ostentatious way that makes him feel embarrassed and patronized, but in a sincere desire to form a good relationship. You'll find it more of a blessing than you think.

In such an atmosphere of self-giving love, loneliness—crippling, corrosive loneliness—simply cannot survive. Rejoice therefore that you are no longer a child of earth but a citizen of heaven, empowered to live the short years of your pilgrimage in godliness and contentment in the company of the Saviour. Like Paul, you are more than a conqueror through Christ who loves you.

Congratulations—you're on the winning side!

About the Author

His home is Atlanta, Georgia. But his international influence touches millions of people because his field of operation is the world. His journeys have taken him around the world more than 60 times, and he travels over 200,000 miles every year. Dr. John Haggai, truly a world personality, is founder and president of Haggai Institute for Advanced Leadership Training headquartered in Singapore.

John Haggai was born in Louisville, Kentucky, the son of an immigrant to the United States who fled his native Syria during Turkey's harassment of Syria in 1912.

A prolific writer, Dr. Haggai's first book, *How to Win Over Worry*, has been a bestseller since 1959 and is now published in over 15 languages. Other books include: *New Hope for Planet Earth*, *How to Win Over Pain*, *How to Win Over Fear*, *The Leading Edge*, *Lead On!*, *My Son Johnny*, and *The Steward*.

Because of his reputation as an informative and captivating speaker, Dr. Haggai has been sought by a variety of audiences. These include the world's largest Rotary Club; the Kiwanis International Convention; the Institute for Human Development in Seoul, Korea; the Texas Medical Association; international investment bankers on Wall Street; graduate students at Yale University; the Texas Academy of Family Practice; as well as numerous other civic clubs, colleges, and universities on all six continents.

John Haggai's face and his name suggest his East-West ethnic ancestry. To the people of Asia he looks like an Asian, not a Westerner. But it's more than a matter of looks or a name . . . he has an empathy for the people of Asia.

Other Books by John Haggai

How to Win Over Pain
How to Win Over Fear
How to Win Over Worry
New Hope for Planet Earth
The Steward
My Son Johnny
Lead On!
The Leading Edge

Dear Reader:

We would appreciate hearing from you regarding this Harvest House nonfiction book. It will enable us to continue to give you the best in Christian publishing.

1. What most influenced you to purchase *How to Win Over Loneliness?*
   - ☐ Author
   - ☐ Subject matter
   - ☐ Backcover copy
   - ☐ Recommendations
   - ☐ Cover/Title
   - ☐ _____

2. Where did you purchase this book?
   - ☐ Christian bookstore
   - ☐ General bookstore
   - ☐ Other
   - ☐ Grocery store
   - ☐ Department store

3. Your overall rating of this book:
   - ☐ Excellent   ☐ Very good   ☐ Good   ☐ Fair   ☐ Poor

4. How likely would you be to purchase other books by this author?
   - ☐ Very likely
   - ☐ Somewhat likely
   - ☐ Not very likely
   - ☐ Not at all

5. What types of books most interest you?
   (check all that apply)
   - ☐ Women's Books
   - ☐ Marriage Books
   - ☐ Current Issues
   - ☐ Self Help/Psychology
   - ☐ Bible Studies
   - ☐ Fiction
   - ☐ Biographies
   - ☐ Children's Books
   - ☐ Youth Books
   - ☐ Other _____

6. Please check the box next to your age group.
   - ☐ Under 18
   - ☐ 18-24
   - ☐ 25-34
   - ☐ 35-44
   - ☐ 45-54
   - ☐ 55 and over

Mail to: Editorial Director
Harvest House Publishers
1075 Arrowsmith
Eugene, OR 97402

Name _____

Address _____

City _____   State _____   Zip _____

Thank you for helping us to help you in future publications!